8.99

ENGLISH GRAMMAR

ENGLISH GRAMMAR

Richard Hudson

London and New York

First published 1998 by Routledge
11 New Fetter Lane, London EC4P 4EE

Simultaneously published in the USA and Canada
by Routledge
29 West 35th Street, New York, NY 10001

Typeset in Times and Univers by RefineCatch Limited, Bungay, Suffolk

Printed and bound in Great Britain by
TJ International Ltd, Padstow, Cornwall

British Library Cataloguing in Publication Data
A catalogue record for this book is available from the British Library

Library of Congress Cataloguing in Publication Data

Hudson, Richard A.
     English grammar / Richard Hudson.
          p.   cm. – (Language workbooks)
     Includes bibliographical references and index.
     ISBN 0–415–17410–4 (pb)
     1. English language–Grammar–Problems, exercises, etc.
     I. Title.   II. Series.
     PE1112.H817   1998
     428.2–dc21   97–34088
                                                        CIP

ISBN 0–415–17410–4

This book is dedicated to my father, John Hudson,
who uses English grammar better than I shall ever be
able to.

CONTENTS

USING THIS BOOK

If you can understand this sentence, you already know English grammar. You know all the words intimately; for example, you've probably heard or read the word *if* many thousands of times during your life, and don't need me to tell you how to use it. What, then, is the point of a book (in English) on English grammar? In a nutshell, to help you to understand all these things that you already know.

Understanding is at the heart of the book. I don't think it will be possible to use the book – however hard you may try! – without grasping some of the principles and patterns of grammar. I've tried hard not to tell you anything; instead, my role is your guide and interpreter on a journey through the important part of your mind which we call your grammar. I will direct your attention to specific patterns and ask you questions, but it's you that provides the answers and in the process of answering your understanding deepens and broadens. I promise that it will work for you, just as for all my students; but of course there is a condition: it will only work if you play your part. You can bypass the thinking stage by looking at the model answers (or skipping ahead), and that may be just the right thing to do in some cases, but if you do that all the time you won't get much out of the book. The approach is called 'discovery learning', and it's widely recognised as one of the most effective ways of teaching.

I'll do my best to help you to understand your grammar. Once you've worked out the details for yourself, I will point out larger patterns and generally try to save you from drowning in detail – a sad fate that threatens every grammarian. I also keep terminology to a minimum – a very small minimum too, you'll find (just look at the index, which shows them all). There are no terms in this book which are there for their own sake; every term is used as a tool after it has been used. And last but not least, the goal of the book is sentence diagramming.

You can get an idea of what a sentence diagram looks like by glancing at the later chapters, and in particular at Appendix I. Sentence diagramming is important because it tests your understanding: you can't do it without some understanding of what you're doing. But it's important for other reasons too. It gives you a concrete skill which you can develop, practise and feel proud of; and it gives you a measure of progress. How much English grammar have you covered so far? You will find that progress is very fast at the beginning, so after Unit 1 you will already be able to say something sensible about half of the words in any bit of written English. By the end of the book, you should be able to diagram virtually any sentence you meet. That's a large claim for a small book, so I must explain what it means. My sentence diagrams are allowed to miss out tricky words, so I'm not guaranteeing that you'll be able to deal with every single word in every single sentence. But I do guarantee the ability to handle all but a tiny handful of the words in every sentence.

My part of the bargain, then, is to guide you as helpfully as I can through your English grammar. You will be the expert on what grammatical patterns you know, but I have to be the expert on how to interpret them, so I shall give you a simple framework of general ideas. For your part, you must be prepared to do your diagramming exercises, to think hard and to learn – there are wrong answers as well as right ones, and I shall have succeeded if you can understand the difference between the two.

In more concrete terms, you may use the book either on your own or in a class, but it is based on my class teaching over some decades. I use it (at University College London) in a class of about twenty-five first-year undergraduates, whom I see for about two hours per week (plus one hour in smaller groups). In that time we cover the material quite thoroughly, and every student can analyse a 100-word text (chosen by them) by the end of a ten-week teaching term. They all make some mistakes, of course, and a few make very many mistakes, but those who work steadily all learn the main analytical skills. On the other hand, the book has also been used in a Canadian university where the undergraduates seem to have coped reasonably well with a much higher speed of about one hour per unit, so it clearly doesn't require such intensive class contact.

How should the book be used in class? Again there are probably numerous possibilities, but my approach is to focus on the exercises, leaving students to read the connecting text for themselves as a reminder of my general points. Each unit ends with some larger-scale activity, which I then discuss in a later tutorial group and which prepares them for the final assessed project. This activity is important for building confidence, but can probably be reduced or even omitted.

ACKNOWLEDGEMENTS

I should like to thank several generations of first-year undergraduates for helping me to build this course. When they were enthusiastic it was wonderful, but the other bits taught me a lot as well. How some of them became so good at sentence-analysis, and with such apparent ease, I shall never understand; but the most rewarding students were those who triumphed in spite of finding it difficult.

Thanks too to Chet Creider, who test-drove the material in Canada. His feedback was really useful, and future users are in his debt for smoothing their way.

The extract from Steven Pinker's 'Language Instinct' is used with the kind permission of the author and publishers.

OVERVIEW

This is a book about English grammar. What does that mean? Before we start I should explain what is in store – and perhaps equally importantly, what is *not*. I'll start with the positive question.

Pitching the answer at the lowest level, you will learn how to draw diagrams like the ones that you can see by flicking through the pages of the book. These diagrams allow you to say, in a convenient way, what you know about the words in a sentence – what kinds of words they are, and how they all fit together. In concrete terms, you will learn to write a label such as 'N' or 'v:f' underneath each word, and to draw an arrow that links it to some other word in the same sentence. For example, here's the diagram for this sentence:

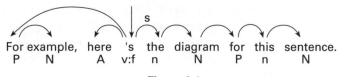

Figure 0.1

This diagram tells you that the word *for* is a preposition (labelled 'P'), that it is linked to the word (believe it or not) *'s* and also to the word *example*; and so on. Even before we start you may be able to understand the rest of the diagram; but if not, don't worry. By the end of the book it should all make sense. But that's only because you're going to learn a great deal more than simply how to draw arrows and write labels.

You have two things to learn: how to classify words, and how to recognise the relationships between them. The labels beneath the words show their classification, while the arrows show their relationships; and of these two things, I predict that the first will turn out to be much easier than the second. Classification requires knowing nothing more than a dozen or so terms like 'preposition', 'noun' and 'auxiliary verb' and how to apply them. On the whole this is quite easy, though there are some tricky problems that we shall try not to dwell on too much. The relationships between words are harder because you have to learn to apply some rather general principles to particular cases. Everyone I have taught has eventually managed to get the hang of it, but some people do find it much harder than others and one thing is very clear: the only way to learn to do these things is by doing them. Practice does make perfect (or nearly so).

If it's going to cost so much effort, why should you bother? Here are some good reasons for studying English grammar:

- You will become consciously aware of things that you have been doing since you were an infant – combining verbs with their subjects and objects, keeping words next to their dependents and numerous other grammatical tricks. If you learned English as a child this awareness will be a new experience for you, but the same may be true even if you learned English more recently. Mastering English grammar was one of the most impressive intellectual achievements of your life, so you have a right to be aware of what you achieved and to be proud of it.
- You will understand some of the basic patterns in your grammar, and catch a glimpse of the immense network of patterns behind them. You should be impressed in about equal measures by the complexities and the regularities, but we shall focus mainly on the simple patterns that underlie most sentences. By the end of the course you will be able to say (or draw) something revealing for almost every word in any bit of English you happen to pick up.
- You should pick up some useful hints about how to improve your writing, such as how to use punctuation more systematically and how to avoid ambiguity and complexity.
- Once you understand how English grammar works, you will find it much easier to learn other languages. Languages tend to have rather similar grammars, even when their vocabularies are completely different, but you have to look for the similarities behind the superficial differences of word order and word forms. At the same time there are also some spectacular grammatical differences between languages, which you will be able to cope with much better if you already understand how English works.

That completes the overview of what you will do while working through this book, and why it is worth doing. What we will *not* talk about is grammatical 'correctness'. For example, when we discuss the combination of *to* followed by a verb as in *to be*, I will not tell you to avoid 'split infinitives' such as *to boldly go*; and when we talk about tense I will not say that *done* is incorrect as the past tense of *do* (e.g. *I done it*). This may surprise you in a book on English grammar; after all, what's the point of teaching (or learning) grammar if not to eradicate mistakes? But our aim is to 'describe' (and understand) the grammar that you already have, rather than to 'prescribe' the grammar that you ought to have.

If you use split infinitives, welcome to the club – so does almost every other English speaker, in spite of the grammar books; so simply as a matter of fact, split infinitives are part of English grammar. And if your normal past tense for *do* is *done*, you're also in very good company because this is the regular, and 'correct', form for people like you, so it is part of your grammar. This is simply a matter of fact. It is not part of written Standard English, but we can express this fact by calling it 'Non-standard', without using the word 'incorrect'. All we need to say is that the past tense of *do* is *did* in Standard English and *done* in (some) Non-standard English; *did* is just as wrong in Non-standard as *done* is in Standard.

If you're a native speaker of Non-standard English then you probably need to learn Standard English (this is just an opinion, but it's one that is widely shared and that I'd be prepared to justify); but being told that your own grammar is wrong doesn't help. Imagine how confusing it would be if your French teacher told you that all your English was wrong! So I'm not denying the need to learn Standard English at least for writing, and possibly for speaking as well. Nor am I denying the need to learn to punctuate and to spell, or the need to learn to write clearly – user-friendly writing does not come naturally, but it is one of the basic commodities in our communication-rich society. Nor am I even denying the need to develop your grammatical skills in speaking; we all know how easy it is to make simple things sound unnecessarily complicated. There is a lot to learn about English (not to mention other languages), and at every turn these things involve grammar. My claim is that the better we understand the grammar we already know, the better we can add to it and learn to use it more effectively.

WORD-CLASSES: NOUNS AND VERBS

1

The first point to establish is that you already know English grammar. Let's consider some evidence. Please answer the following questions.

✐ **EXERCISE**

1.1

Data questions

1. Which of the following sentences is ordinary English?

    (a) Lightning flashed.
    (b) Flashed lightning.

2. Which of the following words may fill the gap below without any other word being added?: like, liking, know, knowledge

    People ___ grammar.

Discussion

I predict that you rejected out of hand one of the sentences in question 1, and two of the words in question 2. If so, you must know English grammar, at least in the sense in which I am using the term. Remember, for me everyone who can speak English knows English grammar, even if they don't know a verb from a vowel.

If my prediction was wrong, then you must have misunderstood my questions. That may prove that I'm not communicating very well – one of the themes of this book is that communication is really rather difficult, and miscommunication all too easy. It certainly does not prove that you don't know any English grammar, less still that you're stupid. Questions like 1 and 2 are actually very odd, and you might even call them a perversion of ordinary language – language turned in on itself, so to speak. For most people language is primarily a tool for

5

higher ends – entertaining, informing, persuading, and so on; the tool works so well and so efficiently that we take it for granted just as we do our other advanced skills like walking, opening doors or tying knots.

Rather surprisingly, perhaps, some people can stand 'outside' their language, as it were, and contemplate it, and for them English grammar may be easy. They are the lucky ones. Their ability isn't a sign of superior intelligence, but of a rather specialised intelligence (like the ability to do crossword puzzles); but it can be learned. So if at first you find my questions about words and sentences unnatural and pointless, please persist and I promise your efforts will be rewarded. You will start to find this perversion a little easier, and perhaps even enjoyable; and the activity will, I hope, help you to understand language and to use it better. Language is by far the most important tool that humans have ever developed, and as with all our other tools, the better we understand it, the better we can apply it.

The activities in this unit are an opportunity to explore the answers you gave, and to work through some of their consequences. Once you have understood those things, you will be well into the study of English grammar.

Before we go on I should tell you the answers that I expected.

1. Accepted: Lightning flashed.
    Rejected: *Flashed lightning.
2. Accepted: People like/know grammar.
    Rejected: *People liking/knowledge grammar.

I have marked the rejected sentences with *, a standard signal for 'bad English', or in more technical terms, 'ungrammatical'.

EXERCISE ✎

Nouns and verbs

1.2

3. The main challenge is to explain why the good sentences are good and the bad, bad. First, can the difference be explained in terms of the meanings of the words? Here is a list of all the words in questions 1–2.

flashed, know, knowledge, lightning, like, liking, people

Classify the meanings of these words using the following list of terms (which are meant to be as helpful as possible); for example, a 'person-word' is a word that means a person:

person-words
thing-words
state-words
event-words

Use this classification to explain the differences between the good and bad sentences. You should aim at an explanation like this: 'If a sentence contains a ____-word and a ____-word, the ____-word must come before the ____-word.'

So what? Can we explain our data in terms of meanings alone?

---

4. Now try an explanation in terms of the words themselves, i.e. in terms of what kinds of word they are.

Classify the words themselves as either nouns or verbs. (In my experience everyone is pretty good at doing this even if they don't know anything else about grammar; but just in case you're not too sure, remember that *hate* is a verb but *hatred* is a noun, whereas *love* may be either.)

      nouns: _____

      verbs: _____

Now use this classification to explain the difference between the two examples in question 1. This time your explanation should be like this: 'If a sentence consists of a ____ and a ____, the ____ must come before the ____.'

The examples in question 2 need a different treatment. We started with a 'frame' of words, 'People ____ grammar.' Your task is to explain why some words can fill the slot in this frame, and others cannot, so your explanation must be like this: 'If a three-word sentence starts with a ____ and finishes with a ____, the word between them must be a ____.'

So what?

As you can imagine, these explanations are not the last word in English grammar; in fact, no self-respecting grammarian would dream of offering anything like them, and we shall very soon have moved beyond such things ourselves. Nevertheless, we have already established a very important and fundamental principle: that at least some facts in grammar are facts about words themselves, rather than about their meanings. We cannot explain the difference between *like* and *liking* in 'People like/ *liking grammar' by talking about their meanings, because they have the same meaning. (If you don't believe me, try to work out precisely what the difference is!) That was the point of getting you to classify all the words as 'state-words', and so on. But this similarity of meaning does not stop them from belonging to different WORD-CLASSES, which is what 'verb' and 'noun' are. Word-classes are one of the basic components of grammar, as we shall see, but the main point that we have to establish from the start is that they cannot be side-stepped by talking about semantic categories like 'person-word' and 'state-word'. This isn't just a matter of tradition, or of belief; it is a matter of fact. It may be, of course, that someone really clever can answer my challenge by proving that *like* and *liking* have different meanings (some theoretical linguists actually believe they can do this already), but until this answer comes we must stick to word-classes. In doing so we shall be following all the grammarians since the Ancient Greeks, who first discovered word-classes.

Word-classes

Separating grammar and meaning may sound back-to-front, given the obvious fact that we use grammar in order to express meanings. In fact, one of the most general points that will emerge from this course is that grammatical structure is very closely related to meaning, and I shall push you hard to use meaning as a guide. Why, then, can't we explain everything in grammar in terms of meaning? The easy answer is that language just isn't like that; but then you can ask why not, and the discussion gets really interesting.

Unfortunately that will have to wait for another book. For this course, just remember that grammar and meaning are closely linked, but different. Here is another exercise to reinforce the point:

EXERCISE ✎

Grammar and meaning

1.3

5. All the following sentences are bad in some way, but they are bad for different reasons. Explain what is wrong in each one.

(a) The earth is flat.   Bad because _____
(b) Red things are colourless. _____
(c) Him likes ice cream. _____
(d) Ice cream likes he. _____

Decide which of these explanations amounts to a verdict of 'ungrammatical', and put an asterisk (*) against the sentences concerned. If you want a symbol to show you disapprove of the sentences that you had to accept as grammatical, you can use '!'.

Let's get back to our main business: the two main word-classes of English grammar (and, indeed, of the grammar of every other language that has been studied): noun and verb. Here's an exercise to boost your confidence.

EXERCISE ✎

Classification

1.4

6. Pick out the nouns and verbs in the following sentences by writing N or V under the words concerned.

Pick out the nouns and verbs in the following sentences.

Children may know the correct word but find it difficult to pronounce.

7. One of the main difficulties in classifying English words is that so many of them belong to different word-classes depending on how they are used. For example, *alarm* may be either a verb ('Loud noises alarm me.') or a noun ('My alarm woke me at seven.'). Pick out the words in the next example which belong to more than one word-class (even if you can't name the classes concerned), and invent an example sentence to illustrate each alternative use of each word. (Beware, there may be more alternatives than you think!)

At times, sounds ring round the resort.

I set these exercises at this stage because I expected you to be able to do them on the basis of 'gut feelings'. I hope I was right. However, even if you could use gut feelings, our aim is understanding, which is a state that's supposed to involve your mind, not your guts. What, precisely, is the difference between a noun and a verb? We shall now try to explore the criteria that you may have been applying more or less unconsciously.

✎ **EXERCISE**

1.5

8. The following sentences illustrate an important difference. What is it?

Criteria for distinguishing nouns and verbs

   (a) Help!
   (b) Help Pat!
   (c) Jo helps Pat.
   (d) *Jo Pat!

Answer: Every sentence needs a ____

9. Another difference emerges from the following:

   (a) Pat annoys Jo.
   (b) Pat knows Jo.
   (c) *Knows annoys Jo.
   (d) *Pat knows annoys.

Answer: A word just before or after *annoys* or *knows* may be a ____ but must not be a ____.

10. And another. This time your job is to think of all the inflected forms of the following words. By this, I mean the various forms that you would expect to be covered by a single entry in a sensible dictionary. For example, the forms for *think* are *thinks*, *thought* and *thinking*; *rethink*, on the other hand, would need a separate dictionary entry, as would *thinkable*. To help you I have provided Table 1.1 which needs to be completed. Remember to fill in either 'V' or 'N' in the first column according to the word-class.

Table 1.1

V	think	thinks	thought	thinking
	idea			
		thoughts		
	get			
				knowing
			grew	
			flashed	
	flash			
	word			
		says		
		sayings		

So what? What difference between nouns and verbs do these examples reveal?

The main point illustrated by these three exercises is that a word-class has no single defining feature, but a collection of them. The words in a word-class may be used in similar grammatical patterns in a sentence, as shown by questions 8 and 9. These characteristics are called syntactic, **Syntax** SYNTAX being the study of how words are combined with one another. But another point of similarity can be in the range of alternative forms, **Morphology** as shown in question10. This is a matter for MORPHOLOGY, the study of word forms. In some cases there are even similarities of meaning; for example, although we cannot easily distinguish all nouns from all verbs in this way, we can at least say that if a word means some kind of concrete object or person it must be a noun. These characteristics are **Semantic** SEMANTIC. The way to think of a word-class, then, is as a collection of words which are similar in their syntax and morphology, and possibly also in their semantics. This is how grammarians have always defined word-classes in a tradition which, as mentioned earlier, goes back to the Ancient Greeks and the Romans. The terms 'noun' and 'verb' are both based on Latin words (in fact, the Latin *verbum* meant simply 'word', which shows how important verbs are – as we shall see later). The only difference between our terminology and traditional grammar is the use of 'word-class' in place of the awful traditional 'part of speech', which was as misleading a piece of terminology as ever existed.

It is useful to know a little more about word forms because a lot of verbs and nouns exist in pairs like *hate – hatred* and *like – liking*. These pairs are useful because they allow us to express (more or less) the same meaning either as a verb or as a noun, according to what the sentence structure demands – to say that Pat hates Jo, or to talk about Pat's hatred for Jo. The relationship between the forms *hate* and *hatred* is unique, but *liking* is based on a common pattern. The next exercise allows you to explore it and others.

✎ **EXERCISE**

**Morphological
relations between
noun–verb
synonyms**

1.6
11. Think of five more verbs which form a noun by adding *-ing* to the verb, e.g. *like* → liking.

12. The following nouns are all paired with verbs that have the same meaning. Which of them illustrate such common morphological patterns that you can think of five other nouns which have the same pattern?

agreement, dependence, exploration, jump, refusal

13. Some of the words in questions 11 and 12 came into English from French and Latin; can you guess which these are, and try to formulate a generalisation about the ways in which nouns can be based on verbs?

We have said enough about nouns and verbs to get us started, but you will learn a great deal more about them in later units. One more thing remains to be done here: to show you a very useful notation trick which all professional grammarians use. Suppose you want to write about a word, i.e. you are quoting it rather than using it in the usual way; how do you distinguish this word from what you say about it? The trick is to pick out the word you're quoting in some way, through *italics*, underlining or 'inverted commas'. My practice throughout this book will be *italics* for single words and inverted commas for two or more words: *the* and 'the book'.

✎ **EXERCISE**

**Notation:
underlining
examples**

1.7
14. In the following examples, underline the words which are being quoted rather than being used in the normal way.

    (a) Students are often poor.
    (b) Students contains eight letters.
    (c) Students is a noun.
    (d) Verbs are important.
    (e) Verbs is a noun.
    (f) I can't stand Sian.
    (g) I can't spell Sian.
    (h) I can't remember Sian.

15. If in doubt, you can always try adding 'the word(s)' before a word or group of words which you think are quoted. Here is a typical passage about grammar from a textbook. Its author uses italic typeface to pick out the words that are quoted, but I have removed all these markings. Your job is to restore them (by underlining), and to check that in each case you could have added 'the word(s)' before them:

> In fact, there are words that are unique. For example, there is no other word in the language which is exactly the same as mouse, with its change of vowel way of forming a plural. Likewise, there are grammatical characteristics of children, good, lightning, say, will and do which no other word in the language shares. Idiosyncrasies of this kind are usually disregarded when dealing with word classes. House is still classified as a noun, albeit a slightly individual one.

We shall celebrate our achievements by building a complete analysis of a short text, the first 58 words from a highly recommended book, *The Language Instinct* by Steven Pinker (1994). (The final analysis is in Appendix I, together with the next fifty-one words, making a text just over 100 words long.) What we have done so far allows us to write N under every noun and V under every verb; if you count the labelled words you will find that we can already say something about nearly 50 per cent of the words. I shall anticipate a later unit by writing 'v' rather than 'V' under some verbs, and to be consistent with another unit I should explain that 'N' means 'common noun', rather than simply 'noun'. You will learn a lot by checking this analysis carefully to make sure you understand it. There are places where you may not yet believe it; apart from the distinction between 'v' and 'V', you may have doubts about the classification of the last-but-one word, *fringe*. These worries will be high on the agenda in the next unit.

MODEL TEXT

As you are reading these words, you are taking part in one of the
     v V   N   v V N

wonders of the natural world. For you and I belong to a species
  N   N   V   N

with a remarkable ability: we can shape events in each other's
        N   v V N

brains with exquisite precision. I am not referring to telepathy or
  N   N   v   V   N

mindcontrol or the other obsessions of fringe science;
  N   N   N   N

SUMMARY

- English grammar is part of what every English speaker knows. To study it we must describe this knowledge as it is, rather than 'prescribing' how we think it ought to be.
- Part of English grammar is the classification of words in terms of word-classes.
- Two very important word-classes are 'verb' and 'noun', abbreviated to V and N.

PRACTICE

1. Find and mark the verbs and common nouns in the following sentence, which (like all the other practice exercises in the book) is taken from a guide to London. (Hint: take *ones* as a noun, and don't pay too much attention to capital letters.)
A model answer is given on p. 120.

It is the contrast between dour, warren-like Victorian

buildings and shiny new ones that gives the City its

distinctive character. Though it hums with activity in

business hours, few people have lived here since the

nineteenth century.

---

2. At the end of the course, you will be ready to do a complete analysis of a 100-word text chosen by you. To prepare for this, choose an easy 100-word text now and find all its nouns and verbs. If you like, you can use the same text in a similar practice exercise after each of the remaining units. Note any examples that worry you, and if you have a chance to get a fellow student or teacher to check your analysis, take it.

2 NOUN EXPANSIONS: HEADS, DEPENDENTS AND ADJECTIVES

This unit will explore the ways in which we can 'expand' a noun by adding further words which modify its meaning. The first exercises focus on one particular kind of expansion.

EXERCISE ✎

Noun–noun pairs

2.1

1. One of the curiosities of English grammar is the freedom with which we combine nouns in pairs. For example, the words *noun* and *expansion* are both nouns, which combine to give *noun expansion* in this unit's title; and the nouns *fringe* and *science* gave *fringe science* in the Pinker extract at the end of the last unit. How many grammatical noun–noun pairs can you build out of the following words? (You may have to use a bit of imagination for some of the meanings!)

> book, joke, language, specialist

2. If a language student is a student that studies languages, what is student language? (Stick as close as you can to my definition: 'student language is . . . that . . .'; but you won't of course be able to use the verb *studies*.) Do the same for the following examples, and complete the formula at the bottom:

joke	book
book	shop
train	ticket
grammar	exercise
jam	sandwich
car	radio
mountain	air

'If N1 means M1 and N2 means M2, N1 + N2 means ___.'

This exercise illustrates a very general principle of grammar: that words generally combine on unequal terms. In the combination *joke book*, for example, the two words do not have the same status because the second provides the basic meaning, which the first modifies – a joke book is a kind of book, and not a kind of joke. An easy way to express this fact is to say that *joke book* is an expansion of *book* – a way of making its meaning more precise. Since *book* is a noun, we can call this a NOUN EXPANSION (and we shall see below that the first word in a noun expansion need not also be a noun). The same is true of all the examples you considered in questions 1 and 2, and more generally it is true of virtually every noun–noun combination in English – they are all expansions of the second noun. More generally still, virtually every way of combining words (and not just in noun expansions) combines them on unequal terms, though this is sometimes less obvious than in the case of noun–noun combinations.

Noun expansion

This principle of inequality among words is a matter for the general theory of grammar, about which this book is going to say very little – our main aim is for you to learn how to analyse sentences rather than how to theorise about them. (Not that there's anything wrong with theory; on the contrary, but I think it's important to get a good grounding in practice before taking on much theory. There are suggestions for more theoretical reading in References and Further Reading at the end of the book.)

All we need for our present purposes are two technical terms and a diagramming system. The terms are HEAD and DEPENDENT. In a word combination like *joke book*, the word which provides the basic meaning is the head of the combination, and the other is its dependent (i.e. depends on it); so *book* is the head of *joke book*, and *joke* depends on *book*. In an expansion, the word which is expanded is the head and the words which expand it are said to depend on it. Not surprisingly, the relationship between these two words is a 'dependency' and a diagram that shows such relationships is a 'dependency diagram'.

Head and dependent

The diagramming system is based on arrows called 'dependency arrows'. A vertical arrow points down at the head, and another arrow points from the head to its dependent (see Figure 2.1).

joke   book
N   N

Figure 2.1

Why arrows? Because the two ends of the arrow (sharp and blunt) are unequal, like the two words that they relate. Think of all the arrows as basically pointing downwards, like the one that points at the head; this will remind you that it points at the 'lower' word – so in 'joke books', *joke* ranks lower than *books*. The reason for giving even the head-word an arrow of its own is to show that this is a potential dependent; this will become clear shortly. (Putting it another way, you can think of it as a flexible arrow that's just waiting to be bent towards one side.) The next exercises will show how this works, as well as giving you practice in drawing arrows.

EXERCISE ✎

Repeated dependencies

2.2

3. Let's look beyond two-word combinations. What happens if you string more than two nouns together? Suggest arrows for the following:

> book collection; joke-book collection; joke-book collection catalogue

4. A joke-book collection is a collection of joke books; but what is a joke book-collection? Or a college book-collection or a lunchtime weather-forecast? Suggest dependency analyses for the last two examples.

> college book-collection   lunchtime weather-forecast

5. If a joke-book collection is different from a joke book-collection, what general advice can you offer on the use of hyphens as a guide to dependency structure? Draw diagrams to show how the hyphens remove an ambiguity.

> joke-book collection;   joke book-collection;

> joke book collection;   joke book collection

You will have noticed that 'joke book' means the same as 'book of jokes', while 'lunchtime weather-forecast' means 'weather-forecast at lunchtime'. In each of these pairs, we can add a little word such as *of* or *at* before the dependent noun to give the same meaning; but if we do, this produces a new group of words ('of books', 'at lunchtime') which has to follow the head noun instead of preceding it. The little words belong to a very important word-class called 'preposition', but there is so much to say about them that we must leave them till Unit 4.

In all the examples discussed so far the dependent words have been nouns. At least, that's how I have labelled them; you may have doubts which I shall try to dispel shortly, but for the present let's assume that it's right. But even if it's true of the examples given so far, does it have to be true of all possible examples? Are nouns the only kinds of word that can depend on a following noun? No, they are not. As you may have guessed, nouns are syntactically rather versatile words – you can use them all over the place, and in particular you can use them as dependents of other nouns. (By the end of the course we shall have seen five other very common uses of nouns.) But there is another class of words which are purpose-built for depending on nouns: ADJECTIVES (e.g. *good*). This is abbreviated as J (its third and most distinctive letter), because we want to reserve A for another word-class. You can discover the difference between adjectives and nouns for yourself in the next exercises.

Adjectives

✎ **EXERCISE**

2.3

Adjectives or nouns?

6. What differences can you find between *good* and *joke* in 'good joke book'? Use the following tests (which later units will explain):

> Test 1.   Can you use it, with the same meaning, after *is* or *are* (e.g. this book is . . .)?
>
> Test 2.   Can you use *very* as its dependent term (e.g. a very . . . book)?
>
> Test 3.   Can you use it, with the same meaning, on its own after *the* (e.g. I like the . . .)?

7. Apply these tests to the following words to decide whether they are nouns or adjectives.

> apple, big, extreme, grammatical, grammaticality, hateful, life, lifelike, likeable, likely, linguistic, linguistics, possible, possibility, pretty, size

8. An adjective can depend on a noun, but can it depend on another adjective? For example, it is very tempting to say that *nice* depends on *little* in 'nice little house', just as *very* does in 'very little house'. Does it? Or do both the adjectives depend on *house*? The following examples give the answer once you have decided which of them are grammatical and drawn the right conclusions. What is the answer, and how does it follow from the examples?

> (a) a nice little house
> (b) a very little house
> (c) a nice house
> (d) a very house
> (e) It is little.
> (f) It is very little.
> (g) It is nice little.

What you cannot prove from these examples is that the same is true of all adjectives, but I promise you it is.

We're now ready to tackle the doubts you may have about classifying *joke* as a noun in 'joke book'. Wouldn't it be better to classify *joke* as an adjective? After all, it does depend on a noun, and that's what adjectives do, isn't it? For similar reasons you may think that *fringe* is really an adjective, not a noun, in 'the other obsessions of fringe science', the last few words of the Pinker text at the end of Unit 1. In my experience some of the best students have these doubts, so they deserve to be taken seriously. Nevertheless, I am utterly convinced that they are wrong. This isn't just a matter of opinion, because there is evidence which leads to only one conclusion. Here it is.

You've just established (see question 8) that the adjective *nice* cannot depend on another adjective *little*, as shown by the impossibility of 'It is nice little.' I've assured you that the same is true of all other adjectives, but you don't have to take my word for it: try to find some combination of one adjective depending on another after *is* or *are* (e.g. . . . extreme nice). If you replace the first adjective by its -ly form (e.g. *extremely*), all is well: 'It is extremely nice'; but the -ly form of an adjective is not itself an adjective, but an adverb (introduced officially in the next unit). So let's assume that one adjective cannot depend on another. Now, suppose *joke* is an adjective in 'joke book' – what then? It should be impossible to combine it with a dependent adjective. More generally, these dependents of nouns should all reject adjective dependents as strictly as an adjective does. But do they? Consider the following examples:

(a) an English Irish joke book (an English book of Irish jokes)
(b) a historical linguistics book (a book about historical linguistics)
(c) a French English grammar book (a French book about English grammar)
(d) a weak joke book (a book of weak jokes)

Examples are easy to invent (try it!). This is readily explained according to my analysis: a noun may have a dependent adjective, whether or not this noun itself depends on another noun. But it's very hard to explain if *joke* and the like turn into adjectives when they depend on other nouns.

EXERCISE ✎

Nouns with multiple pre-dependents

2.4
9. We have already seen that one noun can have two 'pre-dependents' (dependents that precede it), as in 'college book-collection', 'lunchtime weather-forecast'. Is two the upper limit? See how many of the following words you can use together as pre-dependents of *book*, and draw the arrows.

illustrated, recipe, old, priceless, royal

10. How much freedom did you have in question 9 to put the pre-dependents in any order? Try to work out some rules that lie behind the restrictions (but be warned – nobody really understands all the rules yet!).

11. Just to show you that such examples happen in real life, here is an advertisement taken from my local newspaper. Your job is to draw the dependency arrows and to classify the words – good luck! (One principle that this exercise will underline is the importance of knowing what the words mean and how they fit together semantically – in this case, the more you know about car engines the better!) The example actually started with *a*, but I have omitted it for simplicity – we shall discuss such words in Unit 4. Treat the numbers *75* and *two* as adjectives (though I shall question this in Unit 4).

> two-litre 75 bhp single overhead camshaft variable fuel injection unit

Does the analysis follow the rule that adjectives precede nouns which depend on the same noun?

---

12. Suggest a paraphrase of the noun expansion in question 11 in which pre-dependent nouns are replaced by prepositions (like 'book of jokes' paraphrasing 'joke book'). Which version do you find clearest? If the advertiser pays for each word, which version would have been the cheaper?

Question 10 invited you to explore some of the rules of English concerned with the order of words that depend on the same noun. There turned out to be one general rule, which was rather rigid, but otherwise quite a lot of flexibility (allowing 'expensive small book' as well as 'small expensive book', though *'grammar small book' is excluded totally.) There is another restriction on dependents which is much more important than any such rules, because it applies very generally to all dependents (and may even apply to all languages, though this is a matter for advanced research). You can discover it for yourself in the next exercise.

✎ **EXERCISE**

A general restriction on the order of dependents

2.5
13. Why can't an 'English Irish joke book' be an Irish book of English jokes? Draw a diagram showing the arrows that would correspond to this meaning, and do the same for the examples below, assuming that the meaning is the one in brackets. Use the diagrams to give an answer which applies to all these examples.

(a) very expensive small house (target: 'expensive and very small')
(b) mysterious little murder puzzle (target: 'little puzzle about a mysterious murder')
(c) Italian cheap wine shop (target: 'cheap shop for Italian wine')

---

14. All the following examples are totally ungrammatical if we assume the same meanings as in the bracketed examples. Why? Give the diagrams for the dependent–head relations that correspond to these meanings.

> (a) *French old grammar book (= old French-grammar book)
> (b) *home lovely made jam (= lovely home-made jam)
> (c) *historical old linguistics book (= old historical-linguistics book)

The principle that (I hope) you have discovered is that dependency arrows (the arrows between heads and dependents) must not cross one another. If they do cross, this is because some unrelated word separates two related words; for example, *old* is unrelated to *French* and *grammar* in *'French old grammar book', but it separates them. In short, if two words are related then we must keep them as close to each other as possible. The dependency arrows show precisely which words are related to which, and whenever an unrelated word separates two words, its dependency arrow is bound to cross the one that relates them. This is such an important principle that we shall give it a name: the No-tangling Principle.

The No-tangling Principle

Dependency arrows must not tangle.

This is a very important principle for you, as a trainee grammarian. Why? Not because you'll meet sentences that are ungrammatical because of tangling – on the contrary, it is very unlikely you will meet such sentences precisely because they're not grammatical! The logic goes the other way: assuming that the sentences you want to analyse are grammatical, they must obey the No-tangling Principle, so you can be sure that any tangling dependency arrows in your analysis must be wrong!

MODEL TEXT

Here's how the Pinker text looks now. You'll see that we've added three words (the adjectives) to those we can analyse, but much more important is the fact that we now have a tool for showing syntactic structure – the dependency relationships between words. I've given all the nouns dependency arrows, most of which are still sticking straight up, but during the next few units we shall attach them all to other words. A rather small change is that I now start each sentence on a new line and end lines at punctuation marks; this will make the dependency analysis easier in later units.

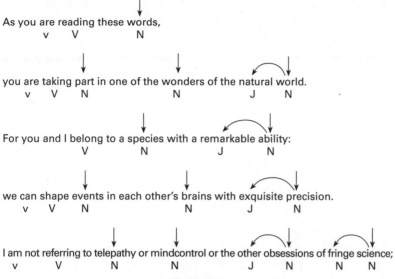

Figure 2.2

- Words are held together by dependencies which link them in pairs.
- A word may have any number of dependents, which combine with it as an 'expansion' which makes its meaning more precise. It is called the expansion's 'head', the other words being its 'dependents'.
- The order of dependents and heads, and of dependents in relation to each other, is controlled by rules and principles. The most important principle is the No-tangling Principle: arrows must not tangle.
- The main patterns discovered in this unit are the following:

  (a) N ← N (i.e. a noun depending on a following noun)
  (b) J ← N

- We now 'officially' know three word-classes: N, V, J (adjective).

1. Find and mark all the verbs, common nouns and adjectives in the following text, and add as many dependency arrows as you can.

This pleasant small square has a paved centre with a

flower stall and fountain depicting Venus.

2. Do the same to the 100-word text that you chose in Unit 1. (If you feel like changing it, do!) As in Unit 1, note any problems you meet.

LINKING WORDS: PREPOSITIONS AND COORDINATORS

3

This unit, like the last, is about noun expansions, but we shall be looking at two new word-classes whose main role is to link more meaningful words together. We start with PREPOSITIONS (abbreviated 'P'), which we just mentioned in the last unit.

Prepositions

We met prepositions in examples like 'book of jokes' and 'weather forecast at lunchtime', where the preposition (*of*, *at*) is sandwiched between the head noun and another noun that is part of the noun expansion. In fact, the preposition doesn't merely happen to occur between these two nouns: it is the essential 'glue' that allows the second to stick to the first. (Contrast 'joke book' with *'book joke(s)', where *book* cannot be the head.) Let's call this the 'noun–preposition–noun' pattern.

✐ EXERCISE

3.1

Prepositions

1. The noun–preposition–noun pattern will do well as a first test for preposition-hood (we shall add another one in Unit 8). English has about eighty prepositions. What are they? (You already know two: *of* and *at*.) This exercise will also give you practice in thinking of nouns, because you will have to vary the nouns on either side of the preposition. There are two things to make sure of:

- that the two nouns are both part of the same noun expansion, whose head is the first noun; and
- that the preposition is just a single word.

You may want to extend the search to word-pairs whose second word is a preposition, such as 'because of', but if you do, keep these examples in a separate list of 'complex prepositions'. In concrete terms, then, I'm asking you to find any single words which can fill the gap in an example like 'I bought a book ____ jokes' or 'This book ____ jokes is good'; and I am (almost) guaranteeing that these words will all be prepositions. The challenge for you is to vary the nouns on either side of the gap and, if need be, other parts of the sentence as well, so as to allow the full range of prepositions.

What is the structure of a noun–preposition–noun pattern like 'book of jokes'? We know that *book* is the head, so all we have to decide is how *of* and *jokes* relate to it and to each other. Only one answer makes sense: *of* must depend on *book*, and *jokes* on *of*, as in the first diagram in Figure 3.1. Why?

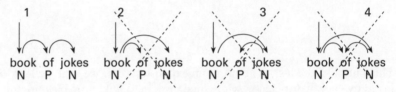

Figure 3.1

Let's take the alternatives one at a time. Diagram 2 makes *jokes* depend directly on *book*; but when one noun depends on another, they must be in the reverse order as in 'joke book'. Nor does this diagram show the close connection between *of* and *jokes*; rather, it implies that either can occur without the other, which is false (think of *'book of' and *'book jokes').

Diagram 3 has the first defect and part of the second: although it shows that *of* depends on *jokes*, it doesn't show that it only depends on *jokes* because *jokes* is combined with *book* – a very complicated relationship. It also treats 'of jokes' as an expansion of *jokes*, which implies that of jokes are a kind of joke – a strange idea indeed!

Diagram 4 manages to have the worst of all worlds – it treats *jokes* as a direct dependent of *book* while also treating 'of jokes' as a kind of joke.

In contrast, Diagram 1 avoids all these problems. It treats *jokes* as a dependent of *of*, which explains why the word order is different from that of 'joke book' (a dependent preposition follows the noun, whereas a dependent noun precedes it); and because *jokes* depends on *of*, we understand that *of* is essential as the glue attaching it to *book*.

The evidence is quite overwhelming, but you may not yet be convinced because *of* has so little meaning compared with *jokes*; in a competition for importance, there's not much doubt about which would win. Just think which you would miss out if you were paying by the word, for example. My analysis treats *jokes* as subordinate to *of*, which (you may be thinking) must surely be wrong? The next two exercises will allow you to work through these doubts.

3.2
2. Should we really expect the head of an expansion to be its most important word? This certainly does not follow from our original discussion in Unit 2 (though you may feel it ought to be added). All we said there was that the head provides the 'basic' meaning which is made more precise by the expansion. 'Basic' does not mean the same as 'most important'. Which of the words in the noun expansions in italics in the following examples do you think are the most important, and which are the heads? Are they the same?

(a) Pat is a *nice person*.
(b) After I'd tried all the books in the shop, I ended up buying a *joke book*.
(c) Pat wrote a good essay, but Jo wrote an *even better one*.
(d) What we had for supper was *Chinese food*.

3. A dependent word modifies the meaning of the head-word so that in combination they are an expansion of the head (e.g. a joke book is a kind of book). What about preposition–noun combinations such as 'behind Pat'? Which word modifies the other's meaning? (To think about this question the main thing to bear in mind is that the meaning of *Pat*, on its own, is a person whereas that of *behind*, on its own, is a place; so the question is what kind of meaning does 'behind Pat' have – person or place?)

Let me ram my point home even harder. Any dependency analysis has implications for word order because of the No-tangling Principle, which bans tangling dependencies. The next exercise will emphasise the way in which dependency relations span the (wide) gulf between deep matters of meaning and very superficial matters of word order.

3.3
4. My analysis explains why some of the following examples are bad. How? Do the other alternative analyses explain the same facts? Give dependency diagrams.

(a) book of bad jokes
(b) book bad of jokes
(c) book of bad jokes with small print
(d) book with small print of bad jokes
(e) book of with small print bad jokes
(f) book of bad with small print jokes

5. In general, *of* has to have its dependent noun (e.g. *jokes*). Some of the following examples support this claim (once you decide whether they are grammatical). Others appear to undermine it, but do they really? Can you think of a way to protect the claim against such examples on the grounds that the dependent noun is there, though not in its usual position after *of*? (Patterns like these are beyond the scope of this course, but you need to be aware that they can occur in your texts. There is no need to try to show the dependency between *of* and the displaced noun in your analyses – it can be done, but requires more advanced technology.)

    (a) I was looking for a collection of jokes, and eventually I got a book of.
    (b) I was thinking of Pat.
    (c) I like Pat and I was just thinking of.
    (d) Who were you thinking of?
    (e) Pat is the person I was thinking of.

Prepositions are important because they are very common, and they allow nouns to be used freely in the expansions of other words.

EXERCISE ✎

Repeated prepositions

3.4

6. How many noun expansions can you build out of the two words *jokes* and *about*? Let your imagination loose – don't worry too much about whether you would ever want to use your examples in real life! At present we're just pushing the grammatical system to its limits. Draw a dependency diagram for the longest one you can think of.

7. A preposition need not depend on the nearest noun to the left. Sometimes it does, sometimes it doesn't, according to the intended meaning; so you need to keep the meaning in full view all the time. Draw diagrams for the following examples.

    (a) students of linguistics with long hair
    (b) books of jokes about linguists with long hair
    (c) books of jokes about linguists with weak punchlines
    (d) books of jokes about linguists with red covers

Before we leave prepositions, we can take this opportunity to announce another very general principle of syntactic analysis, the One-arrow Principle:

The One-arrow Principle
Every word has one arrow-head.

You may have suspected this, but it is important to make it explicit as a guide to your analyses. In a complete analysis, (almost) every word must have at least one arrow pointing at it. (We're about to meet the one exception.) For one word in each expansion, the arrow will be vertical, but for all the others it must link the word concerned to one other word. So every word needs a minimum of one arrow; but this is also the maximum: it must never have more than one. (A more advanced course would say something more complicated, but not that much more complicated.) The One-arrow Principle will help your analyses, because you can be sure that something is wrong if you find your diagram has two arrows pointing at the same word, just as you can if it has two dependencies crossing each other. For instance, you can tell just by looking at analysis (4) in Figure 3.1 that it must be wrong, because *of* has two arrow-heads. The One-arrow Principle and the No-tangling Principle are the only two really general principles in this course, so they deserve your attention.

Now we turn to the exception to the One-arrow Principle, which is also the second kind of linking word: COORDINATORS (otherwise known as 'coordinating conjunctions' or just 'conjunctions'). The main examples for present purposes are *and* and *or*, but you should remember *but*, *nor* and *then*. The list is tiny compared with all the other word-classes, but the members are so common that they rank with prepositions for importance.

Coordinators

What's so special about coordinators? Think of the example 'book of jokes and puzzles'. We know about 'book of jokes', but how does 'and puzzles' fit in? What *and* indicates is that *jokes* and *puzzles* are equal in status, in contrast with all the other patterns that we have considered so far, where words have been related as unequals. This is what 'dependent' means – unequal; the dependent is subordinate to the head. In contrast, *jokes* and *puzzles* are equal in terms of the only thing that counts in syntax, which is their syntactic relationships to the other words: since *jokes* depends on *of*, and *puzzles* is equal with *jokes*, *puzzles* also depends on *of*. The relationship between them is called COORDINATION, which means 'being combined on equal terms'.

Coordination

✏ EXERCISE

3.5

Coordination

8. Let's see how to expand 'books of jokes and puzzles' by means of coordination.

(a) Is it possible to coordinate *books* with another noun so that they both share the same relationship to *of*?

(b) How about coordinating *of* with a different preposition, so that they both depend on *books*?

(c) And how about combining all these possibilities: two co-ordinated nouns, then two coordinated prepositions each of which has two coordinated nouns as dependents?

9. If coordination involves sameness of relationships, it should be possible to coordinate words that belong to different word-classes. Is it? Let's try it out on the pre-dependents of a noun, which may be either adjectives ('big book') or nouns ('joke book').

(a) Can you coordinate two adjectives so that both depend on the same following noun?
(b) How about coordinating two nouns that depend on the same following noun?
(c) And (the crunch) an adjective and a noun?

Coordination is fundamentally different from dependency, so we need a new notation for it which will show both its separateness and its interactions with dependency. The answer is a system of brackets round the coordinated words, and a system for sharing dependency arrows between them. An example is shown in Figure 3.2.

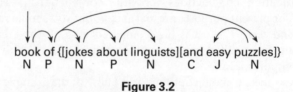

book of {[jokes about linguists][and easy puzzles]}
N   P   N   P   N   C   J   N

Figure 3.2

The main points of this notation are as follows:

(a) The coordinator is labelled 'C', and has no arrow at all (because it does not depend on any other word); this is the exception I mentioned above.
(b) The shared dependency is drawn in the normal way between the nearest words (*of* and *jokes*), but is split to produce a secondary arrow linked to the coordinated word.
(c) The words between this split and the coordinator are enclosed between square brackets: [jokes about linguists]; and so are the ones after it, up to the end of the coordinated word's expansion: [and easy puzzles]. (We could almost equally well write the coordinator outside both these brackets.)
(d) Both the square brackets are enclosed in a curly bracket, to show the scope of the coordinator: {[jokes about linguists] [and easy puzzles]}.

EXERCISE ✎

Notation for coordination

3.6
10. Here are some examples to practise your diagramming skills. Notice that more than two items may be coordinated with one another.

(a) flags with red stars and blue stripes
(b) large red and blue flags

(c) books and journals about grammar (= books about grammar and . . .)

(d) books about grammar, vocabulary, spelling, style and pronunciation

---

11. One coordination may be part of a larger one. Here is a model for you to apply to the examples below. You may find it helpful to number the brackets, as I have in Figure 3.3, to show how they pair up with each other and with the relevant coordinator.

$$\{[_1\{[_2\text{girls}]\ [\text{and}_2\text{boys}]\}_2]\ [\text{or}_1\{[_3\text{men}]\ [\text{and}_3\text{women}]\}_3]\}_1$$

Figure 3.3

(a) red, white and blue or pink (two analyses, please)

(b) red or white, blue, pink and gold (two analyses, please)

(c) red and white or blue and pink (five analyses, please!!)

---

12. How do you think you might diagram the following, showing dependency relationships as well as coordination? Why is it tricky?

books of jokes with red covers and puzzles with blue ones

One more detail about coordination: it allows arrows to tangle even in quite straightforward examples which are certainly grammatical. You can see this clearly in Figure 3.4. What this means is that you have to apply the No-tangling Principle separately to each half of a coordination ('difficult books about grammar' is fine, and so is 'difficult articles about grammar'). This may sound like an obscure technicality, but you need to be aware of it because you may well find examples like this in a text.

difficult {[books] [and journals} about grammar.

Figure 3.4

We have covered a great deal of ground in this unit, so the Pinker text now looks much more interesting (see Figure 3.5). I have added dotted arrows as a temporary link between some prepositions and the nouns that seem to depend on them. The next unit will suggest a different view of these relationships.

MODEL TEXT

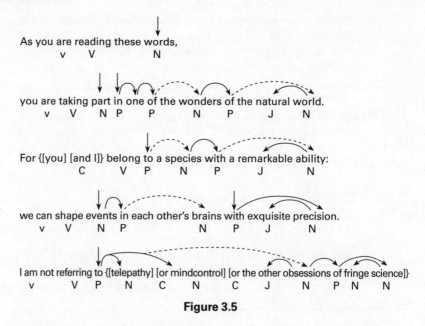

Figure 3.5

SUMMARY

- Prepositions (P) and coordinators (C) both provide 'syntactic glue', though not much meaning.
- Prepositions have a noun (which normally follows) as a dependent. In all the examples so far they themselves have depended on some other noun.
- The One-arrow Principle: with the exception of cordinators, every word has just one dependency arrow (horizontal or vertical) pointing at it.
- Coordinators link words as equals so that they can share dependency relationships. These groupings of words are indicated by brackets.
- The main new syntactic patterns are:

  (a) N → P (i.e. a preposition depending on a preceding noun)
  (b) P → N
  (c) {[. . .] [C . . .]} (i.e. a coordinator between two groups of coordinated words)

PRACTICE

1. Find and mark all the words in the following sentence which we can now classify (N, V, J, P, C), and add both dependency arrows and coordination brackets where appropriate.

This lavishly decorated and well-kept town house provides

a successful brand of luxury bed and breakfast.

---

2. Do the same to your personal 100-word text.

4 SUBCLASSIFICATION: PRONOUNS, DETER-MINERS AND OTHER NOUNS

The last two units have looked at nouns and their expansions, but we have been using the term 'noun' in two different ways and we have left some loose ends dangling. This unit will wrap up nouns properly so that we can turn to verbs, which in many ways are (even) more interesting.

EXERCISE ✎

'Noun' and 'common noun'

4.1

1. In the discussion of prepositions we said that a preposition could link one noun (N1) to a following one (N2) in a pattern that we called 'noun–preposition–noun' (e.g. 'book of jokes'). This implies that the same range of words (all nouns) can occur either before or after the preposition, as either N1 or N2. Is this true? Think of the following words as possible candidates for N1 and N2. (A helpful preposition in this case would be *like*.)

> me, people, students, you

2. In Unit 2 we found that an adjective or a noun can be the dependent of a following noun (e.g. *big joke book*); let's call this second noun 'Nx'. Does Nx stand for the same range of words as N1 or N2 in question 1?

The outcome of these two questions has to be that the range of words which can depend on a preposition is different from the range that the preposition can depend on or that can have a dependent adjective or noun: *people* and *students* belong to both ranges, but *me* and *you* only belong to the first; and yet we have been using the same name for both groups of word. Does it include *me* and *you*, or doesn't it? We cannot go on like this – it's muddling and bad science. If 'noun' means the kind of word that can depend on a preposition, it is simply untrue that a preposition can depend on a noun (any old noun), because no preposition can depend on *me* or *you*. (Try expanding *me* by adding a preposition!)

On the one hand, then, we have a larger class, which does include *me* and *you* as well as *people* and *students*; let's call these simply 'nouns'. On the other hand, we have the smaller class which includes only *people* and *students*. We have already mentioned the standard name for these: 'COMMON NOUNS'.

Common nouns

As you may know, *me* and *you* are called 'PRONOUNS'. What I am suggesting is that a pronoun is a kind of noun (contrasting with common noun). Is this right? The traditional view is that a pronoun is a separate word-class which is used 'instead of a noun' (hence the name, *pro* in Latin meant 'for' or 'on behalf of', so a pronoun is used as a kind of stand-in for a noun). The difficulty with this view is understanding what it means, and how it's different from saying that a pronoun is a noun. After all, if pronouns can be used in the same syntactic places as nouns, and can have the same kind of meaning, they qualify as members of the same word-class; that kind of similarity is precisely what word-classes are meant to reveal. Let's simply assume, therefore, that pronouns are nouns, alongside common nouns.

Pronouns

✏ EXERCISE

Pronouns

4.2

3. What we know so far about pronouns is that they can depend on a preposition (e.g. *with me*), but that a preposition or an adjective (or another noun) can't depend on them (e.g. **English me, *me like . . .*). There are more than two pronouns, of course. In fact there are forty or fifty of them, which can be further subdivided into a dozen or so subclasses. (Most of these subclasses have traditional names; for example, *me* and *you* are 'personal pronouns'; but there is no need for you to subclassify pronouns at this stage.) Here are a few examples of different kinds; can you think of other examples of the same kinds?

   (a) me, you
   (b) mine, yours
   (c) myself, yourself
   (d) each other (treat this as a single word, *eachother*)
   (e) this
   (f) who
   (g) whoever
   (h) none

---

4. There is one important subclass of pronoun that this definition doesn't quite pick out. An example is *someone*. Unlike other pronouns these do allow adjectives as dependents (e.g. *someone nice*), but the rules are very different from those for common nouns.

(a) What's special about the order of the words?
(b) How many adjectives are allowed?
(c) Is a dependent noun possible (as in 'joke book')?
(d) What other pronouns like *someone* can you think of? (Hint: there are at least 4 × 4 = 16 of them!)

Proper nouns

There is one other subclass of noun, which you have probably heard of: PROPER NOUNS, otherwise known as 'names', e.g. *Pat* or *London*. They are certainly nouns because they can depend on a preposition ('with Pat', 'in London'), but they are also different from common nouns. For one thing it is unusual to use them with a dependent adjective, noun or preposition, though this is possible ('young Pat', 'central London'). A more important difference, though, is in the rules for using *the*. With common nouns a word like *the* is generally possible, but only as one of a number of alternatives such as *this* or *a* (e.g. 'the/a/this book'). In contrast, *the* is either impossible or obligatory with a proper noun. In most cases it is impossible: *'the Pat', *'the London'; but where it is allowed, it is obligatory and no other word will do: 'the old Pat' or 'the London of Dickens', but not *'this old Pat' or *'a London of Dickens'; not to mention 'the Thames', 'the Alps' and 'the United States'.

EXERCISE ✎

Proper nouns

4.3
5. Proper nouns are often easy to recognise as such because we write them with a capital letter. (How then do we know when to write capital letters?) But how close is the connection between capital letters and proper nouns? (Remember: a proper noun is a noun which either resists or demands *the*; this is the main criterion, against which you can test the capital-letter criterion.) This list of examples should be helpful.

> April, Bishop, British, Christmas, Frenchman, Latin,
> Mathematics, Member of Parliament, midnight, today,
> Wednesday

What we have achieved so far in this unit is to subclassify 'noun' into three subclasses: 'common noun', 'pronoun' and 'proper noun'. We need to distinguish them in our text notation, so let's reserve 'N' for common nouns (they really are the most common of the three, so the name is a good one), and use small 'n' to show the much smaller members (think of *I*!) of the much smaller class 'pronoun', and 'nN', for 'name–noun', i.e. proper nouns. What about the super-class 'noun' itself? This doesn't need a label in texts (if you're labelled 'N', 'n' or 'nN', you must be a noun); but if we need a label in other diagrams we can use 'N+', with '+' to show it is a super-class.

It will be helpful to summarise this classification system in a diagram (see Figure 4.1). The little triangle has its (long) base against the super-class and its tip linked to the subclasses. Just to remind you that some of these subclasses may be further subdivided I have added 'personal pronoun' below 'pronoun'; and I have added the other word-classes alongside 'noun' to provide a broader view. As their name suggests, these word-classes are all classes of the most general class of all, 'word'. The good news for you is that there is only one more top-level word-class (adverb), and only one more distinction to be made (within 'verb'). So we have already covered nearly all the word-classes.

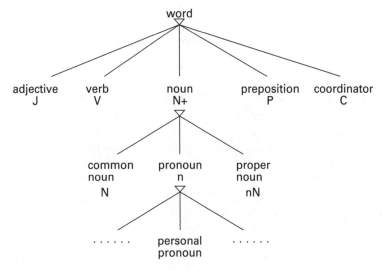

Figure 4.1

So far, I hope, so good. Now we come to a research question – a point where the dust of current research hasn't yet settled (in contrast with virtually everything I have said so far), but which we can't simply skirt round because the words involved are so common – in fact one of them, *the*, is the commonest word in the language, and another one (*a*) isn't far behind! These are the two most important words, but it will be easiest to start with other examples.

✐ **EXERCISE**

Some special pronouns

4.4
6. Some pronouns have a rather special characteristic. Take the pronoun *this*, for example. Not only can it be used on its own, just like *me* or *you*, but it can also be combined with a common noun, as in 'this book'. So alongside 'the name of this' we also have 'the name of this book', containing the same word *this*, with the same meaning and the same grammar. Similarly, its plural *these* can be used either with or without a plural common noun: 'the names of these books' or 'the names of these'. Which of the other pronouns in your list from question 3 can be used in the same two ways, with or without a following common noun?

7. The pronoun *mine* doesn't take a common noun, so *'the name of mine book' is just not English though it's fine to say 'the name of mine'. On the other hand, the word *my* has exactly the same meaning, but has to have a common noun: 'the name of my book' is fine, but *'the name of my' is not. It would make very good sense to merge *mine* and *my* into a single 'word' with two forms, *my/mine*, a bit like *a/an* as in 'a pear' but 'an apple'. If we took this move we could add *my/mine* to the list of words in question 6 which can be used with or without a common noun. Now your turn: which other words in your list of pronouns can be paired off in this way?

Determiners

You have just discovered a class of words that modern linguists call 'DETERMINERS' but which seem to be nothing but pronouns that can combine with a common noun. (I should warn you that this view is controversial – most grammarians think 'determiner' is another top-level word-class. This is a pity, but my analysis is so simple that it would be silly to keep it from you.) The list isn't quite complete – in fact its star members are still missing – but the next step is to work out the dependency relationships. Which word depends on which in 'this book'? It is very tempting to choose 'book', as the provider of the 'basic' meaning – this book is clearly a book. But we can't use that argument as we did with 'joke book', because in that case we were sure that a joke book is a kind of book, and not a kind of joke; so we could eliminate *joke* as the head. We can't do the same with 'this book' because this book could also be described simply as 'this'. So from the point of view of meaning, either *this* or *book* would do equally well as the head. We must consider some syntactic facts.

EXERCISE ✎

The syntax of determiners

4.5

8. Which of the words in 'this book' can be left out?

    (a) the name of this book
    (b) the name of this
    (c) the name of book

Is the same true of all the pronouns that can combine with a common noun? Which other common nouns behave like *book*? Here is a list for you to consider, divided into three groups which I have called 'plural', 'singular mass' and 'singular countable'. Mass nouns name a substance (which may be either concrete or abstract), while countable nouns pick out individual people, objects, times, concepts, etc. – anything, in fact, which could be counted.

plural	books, ideas, people, things
singular mass	dough, furniture, money, stuff
singular countable	book, idea, person, thing

9. Can a pronoun combine with another pronoun, with or without a following common noun? Here are some examples to think about.

(a) the name of his this book
(b) the name of this his book
(c) the name of any his book
(d) the name of his any book

The facts that you have just unearthed show that *book* must depend on *this*, not the other way round. 'This book' is an expansion of *this*, which can always occur without *book*; it can't be an expansion of *book*, because this is impossible without *this*. So why can't two pronouns combine? Because pronouns only allow one dependent, which must be a common noun; for example, *his* accepts *book*, but not *this*, as a dependent. If, on the other hand, *this* had depended on *book*, we might have expected pronouns to multiply just as adjectives do. The analysis so far is the one in Figure 4.2, but we still have to discuss *the*.

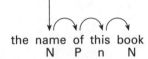

the name of this book
 N   P n   N

Figure 4.2

EXERCISE

4.6

Determiners and adjectives

10. How does this analysis explain the following examples? Draw diagrams.

(a) of this big book
(b) of big this book

What about the most common determiners, *the* and *a/an*? They must be determiners because they follow the rules that you discovered in questions 8 and 9. First, they qualify as determiners for the rule that a singular countable common noun like *book* needs a determiner ('of the book' is just as good as 'of this book'); and second, they exclude other determiners under the one-determiner-per-common-noun rule (*'the my book' is at least as bad as *'this my book'). But 'determiner' means 'pronoun that takes a common noun as dependent', so *the* and *a/an* must be pronouns too! Even more surprisingly, their common nouns must depend on them, just as we found with the other determiners. This is surprising if we expect dependent words to be less informative than the head-word, but we have already seen that this is often not the case – think of the analysis of 'of jokes', where *jokes* depends on *of*. The conclusion, then, is that *the* and *a/an* are pronouns which take a common noun as their dependent. The only difference between them and almost all the other determiners is that their dependent is obligatory – but in this respect they are like plenty of prepositions, such as *of*.

Now I have another surprise for you. If nouns depend on prepositions, and common nouns depend on determiners, look what the effect is on dependency structures. Figure 4.3 is the complete structure for 'the name of this book', which we started in Figure 4.2; but for good measure I have expanded *book* to show the beauty of the system. In this example all the dependencies point to the right, which means that every word (except the first) depends on the word before it. How typical is the example? We know that there are some dependencies that point to the left – for example, all the dependent adjectives and nouns that we looked at in Unit 2 – but it would be interesting to know how the balance is in the whole language. This is something we can do as our analysis of the Pinker text grows (the first exercise gives you a chance to do this), but you can check it on your self-selected text as well.

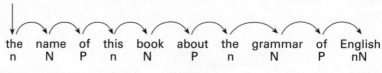

the name of this book about the grammar of English
n   N   P   n   N   P   n   N   P   nN

Figure 4.3

Now that we have our basic subclassification of nouns in place and know how to diagram the main dependency structures, let's look at a few specific cases that are bound to puzzle you in texts. The first is the possessive *'s*, as in 'the book's name'. Believe it or not, there are very good reasons (which grammarians all accept) to consider *'s* as a separate word; you will see some of these reasons in question 13. So there are three words, not two, in 'Pat's book', just as there are in 'Pat's ill'; but of course although *'s* is a separate word in both cases, it is not the same word. In 'Pat's ill' it is a verb (the verb *is*), but what is it in 'Pat's book'? To remind you that *'s* is a separate word I shall add a word space before it in my examples.

EXERCISE ✎

Possessive *'s*

4.7

11. What kind of word is *'s* in 'Pat 's book'? The following examples should help. (Assume that *Pat* is what it looks like, an ordinary proper noun.)

    (a) in Pat 's book
    (b) in book
    (c) in the Pat 's book
    (d) in Jo 's book but not in Pat 's

12. Which word is the head of 'Pat 's book'? Draw a diagram to show

how the other words depend on it. Now do the same for 'the other student 's book' (meaning 'the book of the other student') – careful!

---

13. Why can we be sure that *'s* is a separate word, and not a suffix like the plural *s* in *dogs*? (This exercise is essential for anyone who is unsure about where to use apostrophe's!!) Draw a diagram for the first of the following examples, which are all relevant.

    (a) the man across the road 's new car
    (b) that student over there 's name
    (c) those students over there 's names
    (d) those students ' names

Two other common patterns that you need to know about are complex names and numbers. You could discover reasonable analyses for yourself, but time is limited and anyway I'm not sure what the correct answers are so I may as well offer you the best I have. Complex names like 'Mr John Brown' look remarkably like ordinary noun-expansions like 'the joke book' (e.g. in both cases there is a dependency between the first and third words, with the second word as an optional extra). My preferred analysis is in Figure 4.4, along with my suggestion for numbers like *nine* and *hundred*, which I think may be common nouns. (This is particularly obvious with *hundred* – think of 'a hundred' and 'hundreds of people'; but even *nine* allows 'a good nine'.)

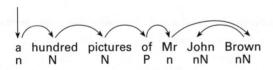

Figure 4.4

Another great leap forward towards a complete analysis. We can now classify all but three of the words (*as, for* and *not*), and we have got rid of the temporary dotted arrows over determiners. The dependency analysis is less far advanced, but we have finished thirty of the fifty-eight words.

MODEL TEXT

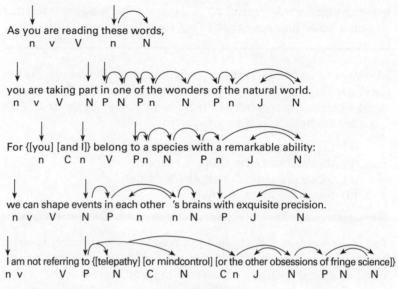

As you are reading these words,
n v V n N

you are taking part in one of the wonders of the natural world.
n v V N P N P n N P n J N

For {[you] [and I]} belong to a species with a remarkable ability:
n C n V P n N P n J N

we can shape events in each other 's brains with exquisite precision.
n v V N P n n N P J N

I am not referring to {[telepathy] [or mindcontrol] [or the other obsessions of fringe science]}
n v V P N C N C n J N P N N

Figure 4.5

SUMMARY

- Nouns belong to one of these three subclasses: common noun (N), proper noun (nN), pronoun (n).
- Pronouns (including *the* and *a/an*) may be used as 'determiners', with a following common noun as a dependent.
- The main new syntactic pattern is:

$$n \rightarrow N$$

PRACTICE

1. Count the dependency arrows in the Pinker text and classify them according to whether they point to the left or to the right. (Count the one split by coordination just once.) Does the result confirm the tendency I pointed out in the text?

2. Do as complete an analysis as you can of the following sentence.

This walk penetrates the heart of Mayfair and Knightsbridge, London's most elegant Georgian residential districts.

3. Update your analysis of your 100-word text.

VERB EXPANSIONS: SUBJECTS, OBJECTS, 'SHARERS' AND ADVERBS

5

Enough for nouns – at least until Unit 9. It is time for verbs. In this unit we shall be looking at various ways of expanding a verb by adding dependents, and in the process we shall meet a new general idea: that dependency relationships can be classified in much the same way as words themselves.

✎ **EXERCISE**

Verb expansions and sentences

5.1
1. Which is the head-word in the sentence 'Babies cry'? Think of the meaning:

    (a) One of the words narrows the meaning of the other. Which?
    (b) Is its meaning more like that of 'crying babies' or of '(the) crying of babies'?

Bearing in mind the answer you chose, which is the head-word?

---

2. Expand the word *babies* (without using *cry*) in as many ways as you can. Then do the same for *cry* (without using *babies*). Which expansions are complete sentences?

The point of these exercises was to discover that sentences revolve around their verb. (What if they have more than one verb? We shall see.) In technical terms, a sentence is a verb expansion, and its verb is its head, with all the other words subordinate to the verb. This is why verbs are so essential in grammar: they are the words that hold sentences together. You may remember discovering in Unit 1 that every sentence needs a verb. As you probably realise, it's more complicated than that (it

41

won't take long to find a verbless sentence in this unit), but this is a good first approximation and again reflects the verb's central position. In short, the verb is the sentence's head, so the structure for 'Babies cry' is as shown in Figure 5.1.

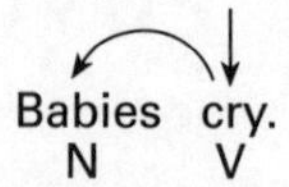

Babies cry.
N   V

Figure 5.1

EXERCISE ✎

Subjects and objects **5.2**

3. Here are some questions about the sentence 'Pat kissed Jo':

    (a) Who gave the kiss? In more detail, who touched someone else lightly with their lips (or however else you think kissing ought to be defined)?

    (b) Who received the kiss? i.e. who did the lips touch?

    (c) How do you know?

4. Write down all the six different orders in which the three letters a, b and c can combine, then replace the letters by words as follows:

a = adores, b = beer, c = Charlie

Which of the six strings of three words are grammatical and express the idea that beer suits Charlie's palate? Why can't they all express this idea? (This is an invitation to work out the rules that relate the order of words to the meanings that they express.)

5. In 'Charlie adores beer', *Charlie* is called the 'subject' of *adores* and *beer* is its 'object'. On the other hand, in 'Beer attracts Charlie', *beer* is the subject of *attracts* and *Charlie* is its object. Armed with the concepts 'subject' and 'object', explain as simply as you can why just the following sentences are straightforwardly grammatical and sensible, out of the twelve theoretical possibilities (six for *adores* and six for *attracts*):

    (a) Charlie adores beer.

    (b) Beer attracts Charlie.

You should also explain why the following are also allowed, although restricted to rather special contexts (e.g. Charlie and Bert both hate wine, but . . .):

    (a) Beer Charlie adores.

    (b) Charlie beer attracts.

Your explanation should consist of two parts: one part dealing with the links between subjects/objects and the 'feeler' (the person whose likes and dislikes are in question) or 'stimulus' (the being that these feelings are 'about'); and another part dealing with word order, again expressed in terms of subjects and objects.

---

6. What other difference do you find between subjects and objects in the following examples?

    (a) He likes her.   (not *Him likes she)
    (b) She likes him.   (not *Her likes he)

He – him and *she – her* are personal pronouns. Which other personal pronouns are paired in this way? (For 'personal pronoun' see Unit 4, Exercise 4.2, question 3.)

---

7. And what about the following examples?

    (a) She likes him.   (not *She like him)
    (b) They like him.   (not *They likes him)
    (c) She likes them.   (not *She like them)

What kinds of verbs show this kind of sensitivity? Try the following examples instead of *likes*:

    hated, hates, liked

These exercises showed the benefits of giving different names to the two noun dependents of a verb. If we call the first one the verb's SUBJECT and the second its OBJECT we can express all sorts of important rules which would otherwise be very difficult to state. The terms are almost as old as 'noun' and 'verb', and have always played the same fundamental role in grammatical analysis. They act as 'collecting points' for restrictions of various kinds – in English, the restrictions involve meaning, word order and choice of word forms such as *he – him* or *like – likes*. If 'subject' assembles characteristics of different kinds, there can be no single definition for 'subject' any more than there is for 'noun'; rather, *she* is the subject of *likes* in 'She likes him' because it has a range of different characteristics which collectively define it as the subject: it expresses the feeler, it is immediately before the verb, it is the subject-only form of the pronoun and it is responsible for the *-s* on *likes*. All these facts are equally central and important. It will be helpful to bring these characteristics of subjects and objects together (see Table 5.1), but I should add that there are several other important characteristics. This table is just to get you started.

Subject
Object

Table 5.1

Characteristic	Subject	Object
meaning	feeler of *adores* or *likes*, stimulus of *attracts*	stimulus of *adores* or *likes*, feeler of *attracts*
word order	immediately before V	immediately after V, or before V's subject
pronoun form	I, he, she, we, they	me, him, her, us, them
verb form	*-s* if the subject is singular	irrelevant

Why didn't we say the same kind of thing about the dependents of a noun? After all, *book* has one dependent on either side in 'big book of jokes', just like *adores* in 'Pat adores Jo'. The big difference is that *'of jokes book big' is simply ungrammatical, because the order of dependents is rigidly fixed according to their word-classes (adjectives before the noun, prepositions after it). In contrast, 'Jo adores Pat' is just as grammatical as 'Pat adores Jo', but carries a different meaning; and if we contrast 'Pat adores them' with 'They adore Pat' we see variation in word forms which has no parallel among the dependents of nouns. In noun expansions we managed fine with the simple notion 'dependent' (though more sophisticated analysis requires further distinctions even here); but even the most elementary analysis of verb dependents pushes us to distinguish subjects and objects. Different systems of analysis make the distinction in different ways but we shall do it in the most obvious way, simply by adding a label to the dependency arrow concerned: 's' for 'subject' and 'o' for 'object'. You can now think of the arrows as pointing towards the word indicated by the label, so the 's' arrow points towards the subject and the 'o' arrow towards the object.

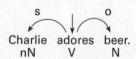

s   o
Charlie adores beer.
nN   V   N

Figure 5.2

EXERCISE ✎

**Prepositions as
dependents of
verbs or nouns**

5.3

8. Prepositions can be used to expand verbs as well as nouns. Draw dependency diagrams for the following examples; make sure you decide for each preposition whether it depends on a noun or a verb.

(a) Pat arrived on a bike.
(b) Pat arrived with a book about grammar.

(c) Pat arrived on a bike with a book about grammar.
(d) Pat arrived on a bike with red mudguards.

---

9. Since a preposition may depend on a verb, a single verb may have several dependents, including the preposition as well as its subject and object; but some prepositions depend on the subject or object, so you have to be careful. Give dependency analyses for the following, paying special attention to whether the preposition depends on the verb or on the verb's object.

(a) Pat helps enthusiasts with their projects.
(b) Pat helps enthusiasts with nice faces.
(c) Pat knows enthusiasts in her class.
(d) Pat finds enthusiasts in her class.

---

10. Which of the preposition expansions in Question 9 could have been put before the verb's object if the latter had been longer? (For example, instead of *enthusiasts* you could have 'enthusiasts who really enjoy grammatical analysis'.) How do your dependency analyses explain your answer?

---

11. Here is a famous joke by Groucho Marx. Its humour presumably lies in the fact that the first sentence is ambiguous, with a natural interpretation which is overturned by the second sentence. Draw a single dependency diagram for the first sentence, with two alternative dependency arrows to show the ambiguity. (In my model answer I draw these alternatives as dotted lines. Treat *night* as a dependent of *shot*.)

A. Last night I shot a tiger in my pyjamas.
B. My goodness, that's a funny place to have a tiger.

---

12. The first of the following examples is ambiguous according to whether *with* depends on *man* or on *saw*. Why is the same not true of the other examples? Draw diagrams for all three sentences.

(a) I saw the man with the telescope.
(b) The man with the telescope saw me.
(c) With the telescope the man saw me.

It will be helpful to review the kinds of word which can depend on a verb. We shall see eventually that almost every kind of word can be used in this way, but we're taking it gently. So far we've seen just two word-classes as dependents of verbs: nouns and prepositions. Nouns can be subjects or objects, but other possibilities exist as we shall see below; in fact, we've just seen one other possible use of a noun, in the example where *night* depended on *shot*.

EXERCISE ✎

**Adjectives or
nouns as 'sharers'
of verbs**

5.4

13. Decide whether each of the following exchanges between speakers A and B is normal, and try to explain any difference that you may find. (You will need to think about the semantic relations between *Pat* and the other noun.)

> *A* Pat has a good friend.
> *B* What, Pat a good friend? Whatever next?
> *A* Pat is a good friend.
> *B* What, Pat a good friend? Whatever next?

Decide whether the following verbs are like *has* or *is*:

> became, knows, seems, wants

14. Decide which of the six verbs mentioned in question 13 can fill the gap in 'Pat ___ pregnant' (where *pregnant* is, of course, an adjective). Do your answers match your answers to question 13? Why? Is this a peculiarity of *pregnant*, or is the same true of other adjectives?

What emerges from these exercises is the need for a third named type of dependent so that we can distinguish objects from non-objects in examples like the following:

> (a) She had a good mother.
> (b) She seemed a good mother.
> (c) She seemed pregnant.

In the first example, 'a good mother' is an ordinary object, but in example (b) it is quite different. For one thing, she and the mother are different people in (a), but not in (b). Rather, what (b) means is that 'being a good mother' was one of her (apparent) qualities, like the quality of being pregnant in (c). The verb's subject has a subject-like relationship to the adjective or noun as well – in fact, we could show in a more advanced course that it's not just subject-like, but it is a real subject relationship. In short, the verb (*seemed*) and its following dependent share the same subject. That's why I use the name SHARER for this relationship. In this case there is no well-established traditional term that can be used without problems (some alternatives are 'complement', 'subject complement' and 'predicative'). The one snag with *sharer* is that its first letter is the same as for *subject*, so its label is 'r' – its last letter, and the one that occurs twice. Here in Figure 5.3 are the structures for the examples above.

Sharers

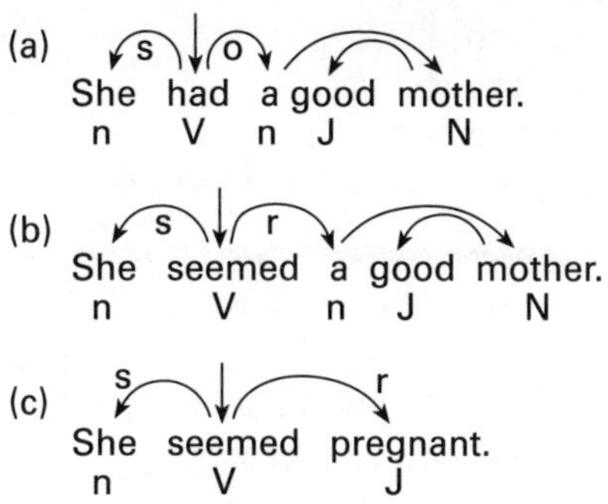

Figure 5.3

Sharers are easy to recognise, provided you can manipulate sentence structure. If a verb's dependent is an adjective it is almost always a sharer; and likewise if it is a noun, but could have been an adjective. For example, 'a good mother' in 'She seemed a good mother' is a noun, but could have been the adjective *pregnant*. What does 'could have been' mean here? It obviously doesn't mean that the dependents themselves have the same meaning, but that the rest of the sentence has the same meaning when they are interchanged: in other words, *She seems* is exactly the same in terms of meaning and syntax in both sentences.

✐ **EXERCISE**

Recognising sharers

5.5

15. In each of the following groups of sentences, one sentence contains an adjective where the other contains a noun (or noun expansion); these adjectives and nouns are in italics. In which sentences is the italicised adjective or noun the verb's sharer?

    (a) She felt *happy*.
    (b) She felt *a* fool.
    (c) She felt *a* drop of rain.
    (d) I got *angry*.
    (e) I got *flu*.
    (f) They grew *tomatoes*.
    (g) They grew *old*.
    (h) He sounded *angry*.
    (i) He sounded *a* gong.
    (j) He sounded *a* nice chap.

16. Adjectives and nouns are not the only possible sharers. Another possibility is a preposition. In which of the following sentences is the underlined preposition the verb's sharer? (You can use the same test: it's a sharer if it could have been an adjective.)

    (a) She felt *in* a good mood.
    (b) She felt *in* her handbag.

    (c) She looked *at* me.
    (d) She looked *at* ease.
    (e) The party got *out* of hand.
    (f) The burglar got *out* of the window.

Table 5.2

Word-class of dependent	Dependency class	Separating dependent	Example
N	<-s-	(adverb)	*Babies* (sometimes) cry.
N	-o->	–	I love *coffee*.
N	<-o-	subject	*Coffee* I love.
J	-r->		We got *angry*.
N			We became *linguists*.
P			We got *into* a good mood.
A	<--	subject	*Sometimes* babies cry.
P			*At* night babies cry.
(N)			Most *days* babies cry.
A	<--		Babies *sometimes* cry.
A	-->	(object)	I drink coffee *sometimes*.
P			I drink coffee *at* breakfast.
(N)			I drink coffee most *days*.

Table 5.2 summarises these rather complicated relationships involving nouns, adjectives and prepositions. The one word-class that we haven't mentioned yet is 'adverb', so now is the time to complete our list of top-level word-classes. As their name implies, adverbs are typically used as dependents of verbs (if you like, you can think of adverbs as being added to verbs). 'Adverb' abbreviates to 'A'.

EXERCISE ✎

Adverbs

5.6

17. The word *quickly* is an adverb. Answer the following questions about the similarities and differences between it and the adjective *quick*.

    (a) (An easy one.) How are their forms related?
    (b) Syntax: what kind of word can *quick*, but not *quickly*, depend on as an unnamed dependent?
    (c) Syntax again: what named dependency can *quick*, but not *quickly*, have?
    (d) And again: what kind of word can *quickly*, but not *quick*, depend on as an ordinary dependent?
    (e) Meaning: are their meanings different?

You will find the following examples helpful, but you have to supply grammaticality judgements.

(a) His quickly/quick running surprised us.
(b) He was quickly/quick.
(c) He ran quickly/quick.

---

18. Think of sentence structure in terms of the positions of subject, verb and object; these three positions define four possible places for other words to occur:

1 – subject – 2 – verb – 3 – object – 4

In which of these four positions can you use *quickly*?

---

19. Think of ten other words which can occur in the same positions as *quickly*. Five of them should be -ly words based on an adjective, but the other five should be unrelated to adjectives. (To give you a start, one such word is *soon*.)

---

20. Adverbs may depend on verbs, but they don't have to. There are three other word-classes that allow an adverb as a dependent. What are they? If you can't see the answer immediately, try the adverb *really* with the following list of words (which contains one example of each of the main word-classes).

adore, adoration, adorable, adorably, near

What, then, is an adverb? When they are formed from an adjective by *-ly* they are easy to spot, but not all of them are, and we have to admit that the class tends to have a rather vague boundary. On the whole you won't go far wrong if you use it as a kind of dustbin for words that 'could have been' clear ly-adverbs (remember, this means that they could be replaced by ly-adverbs without causing any other changes in the sentence structure), but which are not clear members of other classes.

For example, *very* could have been *extremely* in most of its uses (e.g. 'very/extremely kind'), but there is no reason to think it belongs to any other word-class. On the other hand, *today* could have been *recently* (e.g. 'saw him today/recently'), but there are good reasons for thinking it is a noun; for instance, you can use it as dependent of a preposition ('before today') or of a following possessive *'s* ('today's milk'). So we conclude that *today* is a noun (more precisely, a proper noun, nN), but *very* is an adverb.

We can now link all the verbs to their subjects, objects and other dependents. (We can't yet recognise any sharers but we shall find some in the next unit.)

MODEL TEXT

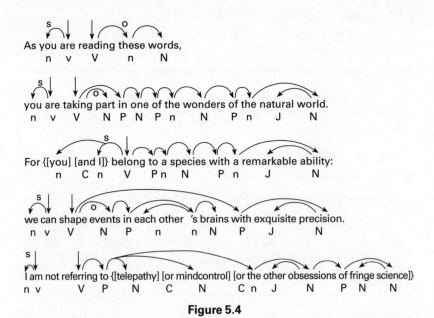

Figure 5.4

SUMMARY

- A simple sentence is a verb expansion.
- A noun may depend on a verb in four different ways, which must be distinguished by labelling in the diagrams: as its subject (s), as its object (o), as its sharer (r), or as a simple dependent (no label).
- The new dependency patterns that have a verb as head are summarised in Table 5.2; we also met the following:

   A ← J (e.g. 'strangely quiet')
   A ← A (e.g. 'extremely quickly')

PRACTICE

1. Do as complete an analysis as you can of the following sentence. Ignore *especially*.

London's traffic is notoriously congested and slow-moving

and bus journeys can take a long time, especially during

rush hours.

2. Update your analysis of your 100-word text.

VERB CHAINS: AUXILIARY AND FULL VERBS AND FINITENESS

6

Most of the words in our model text are now linked up but some are not. There are four pairs of verbs that look as though they belong together, but which we haven't yet managed to connect: 'are reading', 'are taking', 'can shape' and 'am not referring'. By the end of this unit we shall have solved that problem by treating each pair as a 'chain' of verbs, while at the same time opening up what I hope you will agree is a particularly fascinating area of English grammar.

✏ **EXERCISE**

Which depends on which?

6.1

1. Here are the words around the first pair of verbs in the Pinker text:

You are reading these words.

The words *are* and *reading* are both verbs, so one of them must be the head of the sentence, but which, and why? If it is *are*, then *reading* depends on it; but if it is *reading*, the reverse is true. You should take account of the following examples (some of which are ungrammatical).

(a) You are reading.
(b) You are.
(c) You reading.

Should you assume that the head is the word which is more important (in terms of meaning)? (If in doubt, check back in Unit 3 around activity 3.2.) In sentence (b), something is clearly 'missing' in the sense that we have to work out from the total situation what the speaker has in mind – 'You are reading', or 'You are standing on my foot', or whatever. Is this relevant to deciding which word is the syntactic head?

2. Having decided which verb depends on the other, you should be able to work out how to label this dependency. Give your reasons. You may find these examples helpful:

(a) You are silly.
(b) You are.
(c) You silly.

3. Does the same analysis apply to the other three examples in the Pinker text, 'are taking', 'can shape' and 'am not referring'? (Ignore *not*.)

These three exercises should have led to quite a general conclusion: that in a pair of linked verbs, the second depends on the first as its sharer. Figure 6.1 shows the dependency structure for the first example.

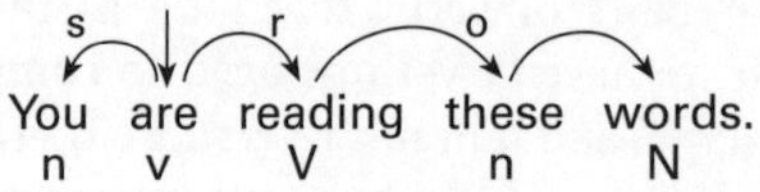

You are reading these words.
n   v   V   n   N

Figure 6.1

A part of you may resist this conclusion, on the grounds that the first verb, which we are taking to be the head of the whole sentence, carries hardly any meaning. The traditional analysis of sentences calls the second verb the 'main verb' and treats the first verb as a modifier – just the opposite of the analysis I recommend. The trouble with the traditional analysis is that it leaves us without a decent syntactic analysis of examples like 'You are', which are perfectly normal English sentences. In any case, the logic is flawed because we have seen that the head-word often carries little or no meaning – just think of prepositions and determiners.

The rest of this unit will be taken up with the classification of these chained verbs.

EXERCISE ✎

Finiteness

6.2
4. The verb *are* is a form of what we can call 'the verb BE' (written in capital letters to distinguish it from its variant forms such as *are*). What other forms of BE can you use in the following sentence-frames? (Any 'form of BE' must be just a single word; a combination of two words is just that – two words, not one.)

(a) You ___ reading.
(b) You ___ silly.
(c) You are ___ silly.

(d) You can ___ silly.
(e) You have ___ silly.

---

5. Are the forms that are used as first and second verbs the same? (You may find it useful to use the terms 'present tense' and 'past tense'.)

---

6. Suppose you replace *you* by *she* in all the sentences of question 4. If one of the verbs is affected by the change, is it the first or second? Why? (If need be, look again at Table 5.1.) What's strange about *can*?

What you have just discovered is the difference between 'finite' and 'non-finite' verbs: present-tense and past-tense verbs are finite, (almost) all the rest are non-finite. This is a matter of the verb's form, which generally means the verb's ending (e.g. *walk-s* versus *walk-ing*). As it happens, BE is the most irregular verb in the language (as it is in many other languages) so its various forms actually have very little in common with each other: the finite ones are *are*, *am*, *is*, *were*, *was*, while *being*, *be*, *been* are non-finite. But the main point is that we all recognise these verb forms as variations on a single theme, which I called 'the verb BE'.

What you found in question 5 was a fundamental difference between finite and non-finite verb forms. *Are* and *were* were good as the first verb but bad as the second, while *being*, *been* and *be* could be the second verb but not the first. Here are some important differences between finite and non-finite verbs:

- Only finite verbs have a tense (past or present).
- Only a finite verb can be the head of a sentence, so a sentence must (normally) contain at least one finite verb, its head.
- A finite verb cannot be the sharer of another verb.
- Only the finite verb in a chain of verbs has a subject, and it is the only verb in the chain whose form is affected by changes in the subject.

You may incidentally be wondering about the term *finite*. This is another very ancient grammatical term, and reflects the fact that finite verbs are 'limited' both in terms of their tense and also in terms of the subjects they allow.

✐ **EXERCISE**

6.3

7. A special kind of sentence is one that is used to issue a command, an invitation, a request and so on. The verb forms found in them are called 'IMPERATIVE'. Here are some examples:

(a) Hurry!

Imperatives and other ambiguous verb-forms
Imperative

(b) Read these words!
(c) Be good!

Why can't imperative verbs be present-tense forms? Why must they be finite?

---

8. English has very few distinct verb-forms (compared to most European languages – if you can think of French, German, Italian or Spanish, do!), but some forms are ambiguous between finite and non-finite. For example, *be* can be non-finite (as in 'can be'!) but we saw in question 7 that it can also be imperative, which is a finite form. Classify the word *sleep* in the following examples as either finite or non-finite.

(a) I sleep well.
(b) I can sleep well.
(c) Sleep well!

---

9. Another exercise to show the ambiguity of many English verbs. How can you tell whether a regular verb that ends in *-ed* is finite or non-finite? Use the following examples for inspiration.

(a) I analysed another sentence.
(b) I have analysed another sentence.
(c) The sentence was analysed well.
(d) I did another sentence.
(e) I have done another sentence.
(f) The sentence was done well.

Table 6.1 summarises the fundamental distinction that we have just made between finite and non-finite verb forms. You can ignore the terms in the second column but finiteness is so important that it deserves to be shown in dependency diagrams. We can add it to the

Table 6.1

Finite-ness	Abbre-viation	Specific terms or forms	Basic uses	Example
finite	:f	present past imperative	head of sentence	am, is, are; take, takes; walks, walk was, were; took; walked be; take; walk
non-finite	:n	ing-form en-form infinitive	sharer of verb	being; taking; walking been; taken; walked be; take; walk

word-classes by a special device: a colon followed by either 'f' or 'n' (for 'finite' and 'non-finite', respectively). Figure 6.2 shows the augmented structure for our first example.

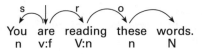

You   are   reading   these   words.
 n   v:f   V:n   n   N

Figure 6.2

Now that we can talk about the forms of the words, we can see that the first word in each of our verb pairs is finite, and the second is non-finite. But what about the verbs themselves? For example, in 'are reading', *are* and *reading* are forms of BE and READ; aren't these fundamentally different kinds of verb? Yes, they are. BE is an AUXILIARY verb, while READ is a FULL verb; in our notation they are labelled 'v' and 'V' because the auxiliary class is very small, and its members are mostly very short. (Think of the contrast between 'n' and 'N' as a model.) The word *auxiliary* is another bit of ancient terminology, but there is no well-established name for verbs that are not auxiliary verbs; the name I have adopted is meant to suggest that these verbs are 'full' of meaning, in contrast with the rather weak meanings of auxiliary verbs. I shall have more to say about the term 'auxiliary verb' below.

Auxiliary and full verbs

✐ **EXERCISE**

6.4

10. How do we mark a sentence as negative? In crude terms, we add *not* or its abbreviated form *n't*, but what (precisely) do we add it to? The following sentences are not all grammatical.

Auxiliary verbs in negation and questions

    (a) You are not reading these sentences.
    (b) You aren't reading these sentences.
    (c) You read not these sentences.
    (d) You readn't these sentences.

11. What kind of verb is DO when it is followed by another verb, and why is it chosen as a way of marking sentences as negative?

    (a) You do not read these sentences.
    (b) You don't read these sentences.
    (c) You don't be reading these sentences.
    (d) You do not your exercises every day.
    (e) You don't your exercises every day.

12. How did Shakespeare mark sentences as negative? Here are some examples for inspiration.

(a) If thou remember'st not the slightest folly that ever love did make thee run into thou hast not loved. (*As You Like It.*)

(b) Dost thou not see my baby at my breast . . .? (*Antony and Cleopatra*)

(c) Man delights not me; no, nor woman neither . . . (*Hamlet*)

(d) The play, I remember, pleased not the million . . . (*Hamlet*)

(e) Give me that man that is not passion's slave. (*Hamlet*)

(f) I know thee not, old man . . . (*Henry IV, part 2*)

---

13. How do we show that a sentence is a question? As the following examples show, there are different kinds of question but (nearly) all of them have something in common that distinguishes them from statements.

(a) Are you reading these sentences?

(b) Read you these sentences?

(c) Do you read these sentences?

(d) Which sentences are you reading?

(e) Which sentences read you?

(f) Which sentences do you read?

---

14. How did Shakespeare show that a sentence was a question?

(a) Is this a dagger which I see before me . . .? (*Macbeth*)

(b) Stands Scotland where it did? (*Macbeth*)

(c) Hath not a Jew eyes? (*The Merchant of Venice*)

(d) If you prick us, do we not bleed? (The Merchant of Venice*)

(e) Sits the wind in that corner? (*Much Ado About Nothing*)

(f) O Romeo, Romeo! Wherefore art thou Romeo? (*Romeo and Juliet*)

(g) Dost thou think, because thou art virtuous, there shall be no more cakes and ale? (*Twelfth Night*)

From these exercises you can see how important the difference between auxiliary verbs and full verbs is. The rules for forming questions and for negation are fundamental, but in Modern English they only apply to auxiliary verbs. But that's not all: there are other differences beside these, nearly all of which have arisen, or at least become really clear, since Shakespeare. This part of English is very new, and some of the details of the system are still sorting themselves out. It's a very good area to look at for examples of language changes that are taking place before our eyes.

6.5
15. What are your auxiliary verbs? Pick out the verbs from the following list which you use to form questions (e.g. 'Are they?') and negatives (e.g. 'They aren't'). The list includes a mixture of present- and past-tense verbs, but doesn't include alternative forms that are found with different subjects.

> are, begin (to), can, could, did, do, had, have, may, might,
> ought (to), shall, should, tended (to), used (to), want (to),
> were, will, would

16. Some verbs have short forms – for example, alongside *is* we have *'s*, as in 'He's working'. These are a very important signal of casualness, and are almost obligatory in ordinary conversation. (You may have noticed that I sometimes use them even in this book; I use them because I want to avoid sounding too formal.) Make a list of verbs that have casual short forms and decide whether or not they are all auxiliary verbs. Are there any auxiliary verbs that have casual short forms in pronunciation but that have no conventional written short form?

17. How many words are there in 'He's working'? Why? Do a full diagram.

18. Is the possessive HAVE an auxiliary verb for you? Decide which of the following sentences you might use yourself, and draw your conclusion:

    (a) They have a car.
    (b) They've a car.
    (c) Have they a car?
    (d) They haven't a car.
    (e) Do they have a car?
    (f) They don't have a car.

(Don't worry if you'd prefer to say 'They haven't got a car'; some of the other examples may be OK for you as well, showing that you can treat the possessive HAVE in more than one way.)

By now you should be able to recognise forms of about ten verbs in your vocabulary as having the very distinctive characteristics of auxiliary verbs. Now, why should these be called 'auxiliary' verbs? This name is traditional, and it is also used by almost every modern grammarian, so it would be perverse for us not to use it; but it is rather misleading, as you will see in the next two exercises.

Historically it was used to show that these verbs 'help' another verb to express its meaning (much as an auxiliary nurse helps a fully qualified nurse).

EXERCISE ✎

The irrelevance of the term 'auxiliary'

6.6

19. If we define auxiliary verbs in terms of their use in questions and negation, do we find that they always occur in combination with another verb?

    (a) They are happy.
    (b) They are in London.
    (c) They are.
    (d) Have you a car? (OK for some people)

20. Are auxiliary verbs the only verbs that combine with another verb (with or without *to*)?

    (a) They kept shouting.
    (b) It stopped raining.
    (c) They helped wash the car.
    (d) I want to go home.

So-called auxiliary verbs have only a loose connection with the idea of helping another verb; they are still auxiliary verbs (by our criteria) even when there is no other verb in sight, and there are plenty of other verbs that are just as good at combining (helpfully) with another verb.

MODEL TEXT

As promised, we can now link the pairs of chained verbs – an important achievement because verb chains are so common. We can also add ':f' and ':n' to the word-class labels to show finiteness.

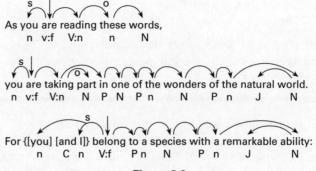

As you are reading these words,
  n v:f V:n   n   N

you are taking part in one of the wonders of the natural world.
n v:f V:n N P N P n   N   P n J   N

For {[you] [and I]} belong to a species with a remarkable ability:
  n   C n V:f   P n N   P n   J   N

Figure 6.3

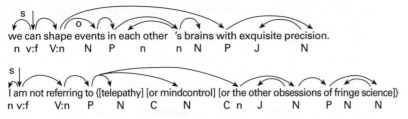

Figure 6.3 (continued)

SUMMARY

- Verbs are either finite (':f') or non-finite (':n'); finiteness is part-ly a matter of the word's own internal shape (e.g. the endings -*s* and -*ing* are sure signs of finiteness and non-finiteness) but partly a matter of how they are used (e.g. a verb ending in -*ed* is finite if it is the only verb, but in other sentence patterns it may be non-finite).
- Verbs are also either auxiliary verbs ('v') or full verbs ('V'). This distinction is based on whether or not they allow an inverted subject in questions and a following *not* or -*n't* in negation (auxiliaries do, full verbs don't).
- Non-finite verbs often depend (as 'sharer') on a verb just before it, and in most cases this is an auxiliary verb.
- The new pattern introduced here is the following (where 'V/v' means 'a verb, either auxiliary or full'):

$$V/v \rightarrow V/v{:}n$$

PRACTICE

1. Do as complete an analysis as possible of the following sentences. Ignore *II* and treat *rebuilding* as a common noun and *designed* as an adjective.

Much of London was flattened by World War II bombs.

Afterwards, the chance for imaginative rebuilding was

missed – some badly designed postwar developments are

already being razed.

---

2. Choose a short magazine article (say, one about a page long) and find all the finite auxiliary verbs. Calculate the percentage that are shortened (e.g. *'s* for *is*). Do you think the author hits about the right level of formality? If you are in a group, compare your percentage with the figures found by others, and see if the differences fit the relative formality of the passages concerned.

---

3. Update your analysis of your chosen 100-word text.

FANCY VERB CHAINS: *TO, THAT, NOT* AND CLAUSES

7

One of the reasons why grammatical analysis is challenging (and why it can be very satisfying) is that sentence structures can be really complicated. One of the things which makes a complicated sentence is the possibility of using one sentence-like pattern as part of a larger one – a process which can be repeated any number of times, allowing any amount of complexity. By the end of this unit we shall have seen some examples of this kind of complexity, but we must first tie up some loose ends from the previous unit which can also lead to complications.

✐ **EXERCISE**

Not and to

7.1

1. In the last unit we saw that a finite auxiliary verb accepts a following *not*, which presumably depends on this verb (e.g. 'was not drunk'), whereas a finite full verb doesn't (e.g. *'got not drunk'). Can *not* depend on other kinds of word? Let's start with non-finite verbs: which of them can *not* depend on, and in what order do the words occur? Try adding *not* to the italicised words in the following sentences. (If *not* is only possible when followed by *but* . . ., count it as not being possible; e.g. 'Not Pat but Jo broke it' does not prove that *not* can depend on *Pat*.)

    (a) *Being* drunk is miserable.
    (b) *Getting* drunk is miserable.
    (c) A *drunk* student was sitting in a corner.
    (d) He was sitting *in* the bath.
    (e) I bought a *book*.
    (f) He ran *quickly*.

2. In the light of your answer to question 1, what kind of word do you

61

think *to* is in the next examples? Suggest a dependency analysis for the words 'try to get', bearing in mind the analysis of 'book of jokes'.

(a) I'll try to get drunk.
(b) A. Will he be back for lunch?
   B. Well, he tends to.

The logic of these two exercises took you to a conclusion which must surely have surprised you: that *to* must be a verb! Maybe an auxiliary verb, and one that has to be non-finite – so a pretty lowly inhabitant of the world of verbs – but a verb none the less. (In case you're wondering whether it's always been a verb, the answer is no; it used to be a preposition.) The other conclusion is that the verb after *to* depends on it; this should strike you as less surprising. Here, in Figure 7.1, is the diagram for 'I'll try not to get drunk.' Incidentally, you'll see that I've classified *not* as an adverb; I'm not too sure of this classification, but it doesn't really matter at this point.

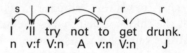

Figure 7.1

Our next step is to look at the way in which chains of verbs can grow. According to the diagram, the chain in 'I'll try not to get drunk' contains no fewer than four verbs (including *to*). Is this about the limit?

EXERCISE ✎

Long verb chains

7.2

3. You may remember an exercise in Unit 3 in which I invited you to build a phrase using just the words *jokes* and *about*. Now we're going to do the same for verbs, using just the verbs *promise* and *to*. If you want to supply a subject as well, do – but it's not essential. Draw a diagram for the longest sentence you can produce.

4. What makes these chains special is that every word is a 'sharer' of the word before it, so they all share the same subject. We don't have to restrict ourselves to verbs for this effect; any word will do, provided it can act as another word's sharer and that it can also have a sharer of its own. This is true of all the words in the following list, which include an adjective. Build one sentence which uses all these words just once each and *to* any number of times, and draw its diagram. You will also need to supply a subject.

able, be, may, seem, tend, understand, want

The conclusion is that there is no limit to the length of a chain if it is made up of verbs (or adjectives), any more than there is if it consists of prepositions and nouns. But as you will no doubt have noticed, in both cases a long chain of similar words tends to be quite hard to understand, so don't get carried away with this discovery!

The sharing patterns that we have discussed so far have all had one word which is the proper subject of one verb but 'counts' as the subject of the other words as well; for example, in 'It stopped raining' *it* is the ordinary subject of *stopped*, but because *raining* is the sharer of *stopped*, *it* also has a subject-like relationship to *raining*. This is by far the most common pattern because it is the one involved in auxiliary verbs, but it isn't the only one. Another is sufficiently common to be worth mentioning.

✐ **EXERCISE**

Object–subject sharing

7.3
5. Identify which is the shared word in the following examples, and decide what its relationship to the preceding word is, and why. Then work out its relationship to the following word, bearing in mind the One-arrow Principle of Unit 3. Draw a diagram for example (d).

  (a) We got them talking.
  (b) I saw him take it.
  (c) They expected me to wash the car.
  (d) You've persuaded me to help you to find it.

You should have decided that *them* in 'We got them talking' is the object of *got*. It certainly isn't the subject of *got*, because *we* is; and its position and form (not *they*) makes it look just like an object, so why not? But *them* is also in the usual subject-like relationship to *talking*; in fact, as far as *talking* is concerned, it is just like *they* in the simpler example 'They got talking'. Since *them* already has one arrow as object of *got* the One-Arrow Principle prevents it from having a second arrow showing this subject-like link to *talking*, but that doesn't matter because we can imply the link by labelling *talking* 'sharer' of *got*. The only peculiarity is that it shares the first verb's object, not its subject; otherwise it is just like 'They got talking'. (It is easy to decide which of the first verb's dependents is shared: it is the object if there is one, and the subject if there isn't.) Figure 7.2 shows the diagrams for both sentences.

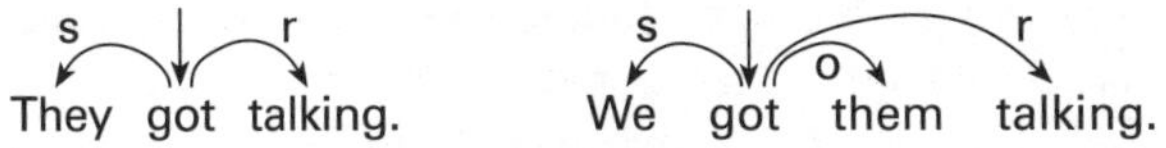

Figure 7.2

This second kind of sharing allows a pattern in which a noun between two verbs doubles up as the second verb's subject as well as the first verb's object (e.g. 'got them talking'). We shall now consider another important pattern which is very easy to confuse with this one, so after introducing it I'll show you how to tell the difference.

EXERCISE ✎

Finite verbs as dependents

7.4

6. Example (a) below contains two finite verbs, either of which could be the sentence's head. Which one is? Take account of the remaining examples (which aren't all grammatical), and give reasons.

    (a) They've discovered she's in love.
    (b) Have they discovered she's in love?
    (c) They've discovered is she in love?
    (d) They've discovered.
    (e) She's in love.

7. Look again at example (a). Which word in 'she's in love' depends on *discovered*? Give reasons and draw a diagram for the whole sentence.

As you can see from these examples, it's not only non-finite verbs that can depend on other verbs. One of the peculiarities of English is to allow a finite verb to depend directly on a verb such as *discover*; without arguing the pros and cons, we shall treat these dependents as objects, labelled 'o'. Figure 7.3 shows the structure for a simple example, 'I know she loves me'.

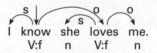

Figure 7.3

Now we can go back to the sharing pattern. The most important thing to notice is that the dependent verb in the examples we have just been considering is just an ordinary finite verb, following the usual rules for such verbs. In particular, like any other (non-imperative) finite verb it has to have a subject. That's why *she* occurs in our example before *'s* ('. . . discovered she's . . .'); its presence has nothing to do with *discovered*. However, although there is no direct link at all between this subject noun and the first verb, the result is the same sequence of word-classes as we found in the sharing pattern: a verb, then a noun, and then another verb. Our examples contain personal pronouns so it's easy to see the difference: *them* must be the object of *got*, so *talking* must be sharer, whereas *she* must be the subject of *'s*, which must therefore be the object of *discovered*. But not all examples are so kind to the analyst.

7.5

8. For each of the following examples, decide whether the second verb is the object or the sharer of the first, and give your reasons.

    (a) I kept Pat talking.
    (b) I think Pat likes you.
    (c) I expect Pat to come.
    (d) I expect Pat will come.

9. The following example is ambiguous; draw the diagram for each of its structures.

    I heard Pat hit Jo.

You probably found an easy way to distinguish finite objects from non-finite sharers: replace the noun by a personal pronoun that has distinct subject and object forms. And of course, the problem vanishes if the second verb itself shows whether it is finite or non-finite. Another way, which gives just the same answer, is to try adding *that* before the noun: 'I think that Pat/she likes me', but not *'I kept that Pat/her talking'. This is a very important word, not only because it is so common, but also because it is a major clue to sentence structure; so it deserves some attention.

7.6

10. We've just seen that *that* can be used before a dependent finite verb and its subject. Is this *that* (see the importance of italicising examples!) an example of the determiner *that*, as in 'I like that idea'? Compare the following examples, paying attention to matters of pronunciation (does it rhyme with *hat*?), meaning (does it contrast with *this*?) and syntax (does it contrast with *those*?)

    (a) I know that sheep.
    (b) I know that sheep sleep.

11. What is the dependency structure around *that* in examples like 'I know that she loves me'? Draw a diagram for this example, leaving *that* unclassified. If in doubt, think of 'book of jokes'.

12. Is *that* a noun in 'I know that she loves me'? Think of the following examples, which aren't all grammatical; if it is a noun, it should be possible to replace 'that she loves me' by a straightforward noun such as *it*, and it should be possible to use 'that she loves me' in all the places where *it* is permitted.

(a) I think that she loves me.
(b) It's clear that she loves me.
(c) I'm thinking about that she loves me.
(d) We discussed that she loves me.

These exercises show quite clearly how we should analyse *that*: as a unique word which allows a finite verb to depend on it. It is unique because it is different from the determiner *that* to the extent of not even being a noun, so we can give it a unique label (why not?): 't' (for 'that'). The fact that the next verb depends on it, although it contributes nothing at all to the sentence's meaning, should come as no surprise; we have seen repeatedly that head-words are rather often short of meaning. Figure 7.4 gives the structure for our example.

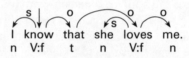

Figure 7.4

Clause

The simple examples that we have considered are the thin end of a very large wedge indeed, which is traditionally called a CLAUSE. A clause is a sentence-like pattern which is not a complete sentence in itself, but is part of a sentence; for example, '(that) she loves me' is a clause because it could have been a sentence on its own (without *that*), but is actually just part of the larger sentence 'I know that she loves me'. There are two kinds of clause, according to how they are related to the rest of the sentence: coordinate clauses and subordinate (i.e. dependent) clauses.

EXERCISE ✎

Coordinate and subordinate clauses

7.7
13. Put brackets round the clauses in the following examples, and decide which of them are coordinate and which are subordinate. (Remember that the bit of sentence which is left over after you have marked off a subordinate clause is not itself a clause; it's just part of a sentence.)

(a) It was raining and we all felt miserable.
(b) I suspect they missed the train.
(c) I hope that the sun will come out soon.
(d) They missed the train but they're coming by bus.

14. Combine the following clauses (just once each) to form as many different sentences as possible, if necessary using the words *and* and *that* as 'glue'.

> you know
> I told her

---

15. A clause can be both coordinate and subordinate. Construct a sentence in which one clause is coordinated to another clause but also subordinate within a third.

As I said at the start of the unit, these clauses are the source of a great deal of complexity in sentence structure; but the art of good writing is to make sure that complexity doesn't lead to difficulty (for the reader).

✐ **EXERCISE**

7.8
Syntactic complexity and difficulty

16. One difficulty that faces readers is misrouting – when the words up to a certain point in the sentence suggest an analysis which later turns out to be wrong. Spot the misroutings in the following examples and suggest simple improvements to the wording or punctuation which would avoid them.

> (a) I know all the students on my second year course in syntax like it.
> (b) I bought a pot of honey and a jar of raspberry jam without pips turned up on the top shelf.
> (c) We all believed the reports about a possible attempt to merge linguistics with physics to be fashionable were nonsense.

---

17. Another difficulty is ambiguity, which leaves the reader uncertain about the intended structure even after reading the whole sentence. Identify the ambiguities in the following by suggesting unambiguous alternative wordings.

> (a) I promise you students will all pass.
> (b) I heard the president put it in the cupboard.
> (c) I can see you like Pat.

We shall look at some difficulties that are caused by sheer complexity in the next unit.

This unit has very little effect on our model text – only one tiny advance, in fact. We now know how to deal with *not* in the last sentence, as an

MODEL TEXT

adverb depending on *am*. We can incorporate this into the next viewing of the complete analysis.

SUMMARY

- Both *to* and *that* are linking words which take a following verb as their dependent and subordinate it to another word (most often a preceding verb).
- *To* is (probably) a non-finite auxiliary verb, and *that* is unique and therefore unclassifiable (labelled 't').
- If a verb has an object as well as a sharer (e.g. 'get them talking'), the object doubles up as the sharer's subject; otherwise, the sharer's subject is also the first verb's subject (e.g. 'get talking').
- A clause is a sentence-like sentence-part. Complicated sentence-structure tends to involve multiple clauses.
- New syntactic patterns:

  (a) to   → V+:n (e.g. 'to come')
  (b) t   → V+:f (e.g. 'that (she) likes')
  (c) V+ → V+:f (e.g. 'know (she) likes')
  (d) V+ → t (e.g. 'know that (she likes)')

PRACTICE

1. Do as complete an analysis as you can of the following. Notice how I break the lines at points where there is a natural break in the syntax, even if this means a short line.

The Garrick is heavily atmospheric

and the ghost of Arthur Bouchier is reputed

to make fairly regular appearances.

He hated critics and many believe

he is still trying to frighten them away.

2. Update your analysis of your 100-word text.

SUBORDINATE CLAUSE CLUES: WH-PRONOUNS, PREPOSITIONS AND NON-FINITE VERBS (AGAIN)

8

Only two words in our model text still remain unanalysed: *as* and *for*; but we shall need all the remaining three units to deal with them. Why so much fuss over two words? (And such tiny words, at that!) Because they will give us an opportunity to go more thoroughly into subordinate clauses, which I flagged as a particularly tricky part of grammatical analysis in Unit 7. They will even give us a peg on which to hang a discussion of the notion 'sentence' in the very last unit. In this unit we focus on the relationships between these words and the subordinate clauses that they introduce, while the next unit will discuss the ways in which they plus their subordinate clause fit into the larger sentence. As it happens, *as* and *for* are both slightly tricky, so we shall look at some easier words first and come back to these later.

✐ EXERCISE

Prepositions

8.1

1. The preposition *after* can be used either before a noun (e.g. 'after midnight') or before a finite verb and this verb's subject (e.g. 'after I saw her'); but its meaning is basically the same in both patterns ('a time earlier than the time of X', where X is the time of the following noun or verb). How many other prepositions can be used in both ways, without change of meaning? (There is an almost complete list of single-word prepositions in the model answer to question 1 of Unit 3. Make sure your examples accept a finite verb – non-finite verbs like *seeing* are possible with a lot of prepositions, but irrelevant for present purposes.)

2. What do you think is the best analysis for 'after I saw her'? Specifically, what word-class does *after* belong to, and how does it fit into the dependency structure? Take account of the following facts and give reasons.

- Prepositions like *after* have the same meaning whether they are followed by a noun or by a finite verb.
- In both patterns the following word supplies the time with which the 'before' time is compared.
- The noun that follows a preposition depends on it.
- Our definition of 'preposition' in Unit 3 just says that its dependent can be a noun; but we had no reason at that stage to think that its dependent had to be a noun.

This evidence suggests that when a word like *after* is followed by a finite verb (as in 'after I saw her') the dependency structure is the same as with *that*, which we looked at in the last unit: *after/that* has a following finite verb depending on it. Its presence signals that a subordinate clause is going to follow; or in more traditional terms, it 'introduces a subordinate clause'. The example in Figure 8.1 contains two subordinate clauses, one inside the other ('I left' contained within 'she arrived after I left'). Please notice that there is still no reason to think that *after* and *that* belong to the same word-class: one is a preposition, while the other is simply unclassifiable. Nor are we saying that *after* has as little meaning as *that*; on the contrary, it has just as much meaning – in fact, the same meaning – whether its dependent is a noun or a verb. All they have in common is the possibility of introducing a subordinate clause.

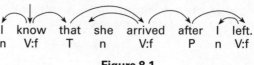

Figure 8.1

This analysis of 'after I left' is very satisfying, as it reveals two partial similarities: on the one hand, to 'after midnight', and on the other hand to 'that I left'. Like any other good thing, though, it has a cost. The price we pay for it is a more complicated definition of 'preposition'. We are now allowing not only nouns but also finite verbs as dependents of prepositions. We shall see below that even further possibilities have to be envisaged; but this just brings prepositions into line with verbs, which allow all sorts of other word-classes as dependents. (Think of the verb *believe*, for example: just like *after* it allows either a noun or a finite verb as its object: 'believe the story' or 'believe she likes me', but we wouldn't dream of putting *believe* into two different word-classes in these two cases.)

We now have two kinds of preposition:

- Those like *of* and *with* that allow only nouns as their dependent.

- Those like *after* and *since* that allow either a noun or a finite verb.

But having recognised these two possibilities, why not a third?

- Those like *if* and *because* which allow a finite verb but not a noun as in the following examples:

(a) We get wet if/because it rains.
(b) *We get wet if/because bad weather.

✐ **EXERCISE**

Prepositions introducing subordinate clauses

8.2

3. Find some more prepositions in the following list.

(al)though, because, but, even, if, never, once, soon, though, wheel, when, where, whereas, while, whim

---

4. Draw diagrams for the following sentences, and decide how you know which verb depends on the preposition and which one the preposition depends on. (More on the alternative orders in the next unit.)

(a) After the rain we had a walk.
(b) After it rained we had a walk.
(c) We had a walk after it rained.

---

5. Apply your answer for question 4 to the first unanalysed preposition in the Pinker text, *as*. Which word depends on it?

As you are reading these words, you are taking part . . .

---

6. Now do the same for the second unanalysed preposition: which word depends on *for*?

. . . you are taking part. . . . For you and I belong to a species . . .: we can shape . . .

To summarise, we have considered two kinds of word that can introduce a subordinate clause: *that* or a preposition. (Why isn't *that* also a preposition? Because it doesn't behave at all like one, as we shall see in the next unit.) This isn't the end, but the list doesn't go on for ever – there are just two other general possibilities that you should be aware of.

EXERCISE ✎

Wh-pronouns

8.3

7. Which word-class does *what* belong to? What's special about it, and which other words have the same combination of characteristics? Draw a diagram for example (b) and comment on any problems.

> (a) What happened?
> (b) What is he eating it with?

---

8. What kind of word can be the object of *ask*? Take account of the following examples – not all of which are grammatical! (Assume that *whether* and *if* are pronouns; this is controversial, and almost certainly wrong for *if*, but not important.)

> (a) We asked Pat.
> (b) We asked a question.
> (c) We asked what happened.
> (d) We asked whether/if it happened.
> (e) We asked it happened.

---

9. Use your answer to question 8 in order to work out the structure of example (c), 'We asked what happened', and draw a diagram for it. Why is the relationship between *what* and *happened* problematic?

The words you found in question 7 are all pronouns, and you won't be surprised to hear that they are called 'wh-pronouns'. These are of great interest to theoreticians because they break some important general principles. In particular, they normally occur at the beginning of their clause rather than in the position where other pronouns would have occurred, which produces various kinds of tangled and multiple dependencies. We shall ignore these problems in this course, but they need attention in any serious discussion of grammar. In your own analyses, just follow the model analyses that I have given, making sure that each word has just a single arrow and that arrows don't tangle. Wh-pronouns, then, are the third type of word that can introduce a subordinate clause. Figure 8.2 shows the analysis of a straightforward example.

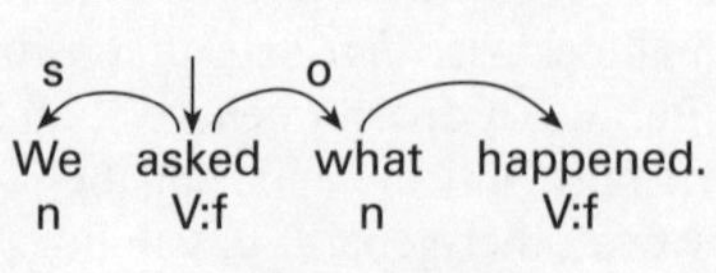

We   asked   what   happened.
n   V:f   n   V:f

Figure 8.2

✐ EXERCISE

Wh-pronouns or prepositions?

8.4
10. You may have noticed that the list of prepositions in question 3 included four words that started with *wh*: *when, where, whereas, while.* Could any of these have been classified as wh-pronouns instead? (Remember, what wh-pronouns had in common was that they could be used to introduce a clause after a verb such as *ask*.) Nevertheless, there is also evidence that these words are prepositions. How do the following examples (some of which are not grammatical) show this?

(a) Pat whistles while/when working.
(b) If/where possible, you should avoid long sentences.
(c) I asked who working.

One detail is quite intriguing: *when* and *where* are clearly wh-pronouns in some uses, but equally clearly prepositions in others. This is good news for you, because it means you can generally get away with either analysis!

One of the things which makes wh-pronouns different from prepositions as introducers of subordinate clauses is that the wh-pronoun doesn't just signal the start of the clause and how it is related to the rest of the sentence: it actually takes part in the subordinate clause's internal structure. This is what we found in 'We asked what happened': *what* is the subject of *happened*, so the subordinate clause is 'what happened', with *what* firmly integrated. In some cases the same may be true of *that*, though this is controversial and you can ignore it – just label *that* as 't' (I am thinking of examples like 'the thing that happened', where *that* again looks like the subject of *happened*). In contrast, a preposition like *if* or *while* is in no sense a part of the clause that it introduces; for example, in 'We get wet if it rains', *if* simply helps the meaning of 'it rains' to modify the meaning of 'we get wet'.

The fourth type of clause-introducer is even more tightly integrated into the clause's structure than wh-pronouns are: it is the clause's very own verb, whose form shows that it is dependent. Once again we have to distinguish clearly between finite and non-finite verbs.

✐ EXERCISE

Non-finite subordinate clauses

8.5
11. The easiest non-finite form of a verb is the one that ends in *ing* (for every verb), as in *driving, being,* and so on; this form, which is often called the ing-form, is used to signal a subordinate clause (of which it is usually the first word), for example, 'driving fast cars', 'being a mere linguist'. You can often save words by using such a clause instead of one introduced by *that*, a preposition or a wh-pronoun with little or no change to the meaning. Do this in the following examples.

(a) I like books that contain really obscure grammatical constructions.

(b) As I walked down the road last night I had a brilliant idea.

(c) People who live in glass houses shouldn't throw stones.

---

12. A second non-finite form which is fairly easy to recognise may have the distinctive ending *en* (as in *driven*, *been*), but it generally looks (and sounds) like a past-tense finite form (e.g. *bought*, *put* and all the regular verbs such as *walked* and *analysed*). In both cases it is called the verb's en-form. Like the ing-form this one can introduce a subordinate clause with much the same meaning as a longer one introduced by a separate word. Make this change to the following sentences. (You will need to make several changes to sentences (c) and (d).)

(a) Books that were published before 1970 tended to have hard covers.

(b) The potatoes tasted nice when they were baked in the ashes of the fire.

(c) If you drive it carefully, this car will outlast you.

(d) We wrote to all the students whom we selected to give seminars.

---

13. The third non-finite form (the infinitive) always looks just like an imperative (which is of course a kind of finite verb) – *be*, *come*, *drive*, *walk*, and so on. This form is generally used in combination with some other verb – 'will be', 'can come' and so on, including (believe it or not) the 'verb' *to*: 'to be', 'to come' (see Unit 7). The combination of *to* plus a non-finite verb may once again be a short alternative to a full subordinate clause introduced by *that*, a preposition or a wh-pronoun. Make the necessary changes to the following examples.

(a) I hope that I'll see you soon.

(b) I did it so that I would please you.

(c) I bought a book which I can read on the train.

(d) A good book which you might read is this one.

Figure 8.3 shows a typical non-finite verb introducing a subordinate clause. These non-finite verbs overlap with the ones that we looked at in Units 6 and 7, where they featured as sharers of verbs (especially auxiliary verbs). For example, *to* in 'I hope to see you soon' is the sharer

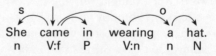

Figure 8.3

of *hope*, with *see* as its own sharer. The logic is that 'to see you soon' is one subordinate clause, while 'see you soon' is another – and 'working hard' is a subordinate clause in 'She is working hard'. If you don't feel comfortable with this conclusion, it doesn't really matter because the term 'subordinate clause' isn't in fact part of the sentence analyses you are learning here. All you have to show are the dependency arrows; traditionally some groups of words that are held together by dependencies are picked out for special mention as 'subordinate clauses', but the term has never been clearly defined and we don't need to define it clearly now.

The main point is that there are just four ways of signalling that a verb-headed group (a 'clause') is dependent on other words, which we have reviewed in this unit. They are summarised in Table 8.1. The examples in this table contain brackets round the subordinate clause and its 'signal'.

Table 8.1

Signal of dependency	Form of verb	Example
that	finite	I think [that she likes you]. The books [that I bought] were cheap.
preposition	finite	She laughs [if he tickles her]. We left [before it rained].
wh-pronoun	finite or *to*	I asked [what she wanted]. We wondered [when to leave]. The books [which I bought] were cheap.
non-finite verb	ing-form, en-form, infinitive, *to*	I asked [to see her]. He returned [covered in mud]. I walked [to keep warm].

✏ **EXERCISE**

A complicated pattern

8.6

14. There is one extra twist that you should be aware of because it is quite likely to appear in any text that you analyse. In a nutshell, some prepositions can have not one, but two, dependents, one of which is a non-finite verb while the other is this verb's subject. See if you can find examples of this pattern in the following examples and try to draw diagrams.

(a) He went to work with it hanging out.
(b) We're hoping for it to rain.

MODEL TEXT

Our main achievement in this unit is to link the prepositions *as* and *for* to their dependent verbs, *are* and *belong*; so we now know that *as* introduces the clause 'you are reading these words', and *for* introduces 'you and I belong to a species'. This is what you did in questions 5 and 6. There is no point in reprinting the whole text until we can also show which words *as* and *for* themselves depend on. We shall be able to do this at the end of the next unit.

SUMMARY

- Subordinate clauses may be identified as such by four kinds of 'signal', which are summarised in Table 8.1: *that*, prepositions, wh-pronouns or the verb's own non-finite form (or *to*). (These are the 'new syntactic patterns' for this unit.)
- In each of these four patterns, the signal word (almost always) stands before the rest of the clause, and in every case the clause's head verb either is the clue, or depends on it.
- Wh-pronouns raise especially tricky problems for the theory of grammar because they also double up as dependents of the subordinate verb. You have to ignore these extra dependencies in your analyses.

PRACTICE

1. Do as complete an analysis as you can of the following. Officially you don't yet know how to link subordinate clauses to the words outside them, but some of these links should be obvious now. The next unit will give more help.

This is one of three nineteenth-century arcades

of small shops selling traditional British luxuries.

It was built for Lord Cavendish in 1819

to stop passers-by throwing rubbish into his garden.

The arcade is still patrolled by beadles

who ensure that decorum is maintained.

2. The usual: update the analysis of your 100-word text.

SUBORDINATE CLAUSE USES

9

To summarise the story so far, verb expansions are called either 'sentences' or 'clauses' according to whether or not they are complete (in a sense that we have taken for granted so far but which we shall look at rather harder in the next unit). Two (or more) clauses may be coordinated without any subordination (e.g. 'It rained and we got wet') but we are concerned in this unit with the ones that are subordinated to some word in the larger sentence. Whereas Unit 8 looked at the 'signal' words which introduce subordinate clauses, in this unit we are going to consider the various possible relations between the subordinate clause and the rest of the sentence.

Once again the signal words will turn out to be the key to the discussion, because they are generally the words which are directly involved in these external relations. For example:

> Because it rained we got wet.

Loosely speaking the clause 'because it rained' is subordinate to the clause 'we got wet'; but that really is very loose talk. More precisely, we shall find that the word *because* depends on the word *got*, and that the word *rained* depends on the word *because* – in other words, there is a chain of dependencies:

> *got → because → rained.*

9.1

1. Suggest dependency diagrams for the following sentences, bearing in mind what we found in the last two units. Make sure that every word has one arrow.

✎ **EXERCISE**

Subordinate clauses as subjects and objects: noun clauses

(a) I know she loves me.
(b) That she loves me is beyond doubt.
(c) Why she loves me baffles me.

---

2. Subordinate clauses aren't always as easy as this. Let's start by creating our own complexities. Using the following words, build a subordinate clause which could be the subject of *is* in '. . . isn't clear'. (Hint: start by finding a word which could introduce this clause, then the finite verb you expect after this word, then this verb's expected subject and other expected dependents, and so on.)

alive all are day debt getting hours how into of or stay
students supposed the to without working

---

3. Now for some real live examples, in which other kinds of subordinate clause are mixed up with those that are subjects or objects. Don't try to draw diagrams for these examples – concentrate on picking out the subordinate clauses and their signals. Follow the model of the worked example, where I have put square brackets round each subordinate clause and its signal word, with the latter in italics.

They claimed [the Tories *had* quietly backed off the scheme [*because* it is badly frightening 'switcher' pensioners]].

Ignore 'clauses' whose head depends on an auxiliary verb. Good luck – and don't panic when the brackets pile up!

(a) Why South Africans hold that the possibility of such negative beliefs is so strong they have to be denied remains to be seen.
(b) That the higher degree of noun plural marking when preceded by a quantifier is not peculiar to the acquisition of English by speakers with a Chinese language background is shown in Sudipa's investigation of essays written in English by students at Udayana University, Bali.
(c) You don't have to be an economic genius to see that what the economy needs is an increase in taxation to solve the twin problems of a rising budget deficit and booming consumer spending (which will be aggravated after the election when building society windfalls are spent).

The subordinate clauses that you focused on in questions 1–3 are subjects or objects, which is a typical use for nouns; and in many cases the clause could have been replaced by a noun; for example we could reduce example (a) above to 'That remains to be seen', where *that* stands for the whole clause 'Why South Africans hold that the possibility of such negative beliefs is so strong that they have to be denied'.

Because of this similarity to nouns linguists often call such subordinate clauses NOUN CLAUSES. We already know (from Units 7 and 8) how to diagram such sentences but they are important as evidence that a verb expansion (in this case, a subordinate clause) is no different from a noun expansion in its ability to act as a dependent of a single word, a verb.

Noun clauses

The examples also showed that there are important differences between external and internal relationships – between function and structure. What noun clauses have in common is their noun-like function, not their structure. If we think of a clause's structure in terms of the 'signal' words that we discussed in the last unit, the structures available for noun clauses illustrate all the general types: no signal at all, *that*, preposition, wh-pronoun, non-finite verb. These structural options are illustrated in the next examples.

(a) I expect [you can analyse this example].   zero
(b) They promised [*that* we would arrive in time].   *that*
(c) I'm longing [*for* it to get warmer].   preposition
(d) Nobody knows [*who* did it].   wh-pronoun
(e) [*To* make mistakes] is natural.   non-finite verb

✎ **EXERCISE**

9.2
4. Subordinate clauses can also be used in ways very similar to adjectives, as part of a noun expansion. For example, the next three sentences all express the same meaning although the part that changes is an adjective in one sentence and a subordinate clause in the others.

Subordinate clauses as modifiers of nouns: relative clauses

(a) I can't afford *expensive* books.
(b) I can't afford books [that are expensive].
(c) I can't afford books [that cost a lot].

What adjectives could be used instead of the subordinate clauses in the following noun expansions?

(a) students who are keen
(b) students who know nothing
(c) students who arrive late
(d) students who they have rejected
(e) students who many people like (careful!)

5. What other structures would have been possible to express the same *meaning* as the subordinate clause in the following? (Organise your answer round the list of five general structures illustrated above.)

I enjoyed the book [that they recommended].

6. Draw dependency diagrams for the example in question 5) and the alternatives that you found. Remember that the subordinate clause's signal word is the one that links it to the rest of the sentence, so all you have to do, once you've found the signal word, is to decide which other word this depends on. If there is no signal word, take the subordinate clause's head verb.

---

7. The structures available for these subordinate clauses overlap considerably with those for noun clauses, which can give rise to ambiguity. Each of the following sentences contains a subordinate clause which could be taken either as a noun clause or as one functioning like an adjective. Draw two diagrams for each sentence showing these two possibilities, with the noun clause analysis first.

(a) I told the students who had passed.
(b) We warned everyone that we were interviewing.

Relative clause

The obvious name for subordinate clauses that are used like adjectives would be 'adjective clauses', and the term 'adjectival clause' is in fact sometimes used; but their established traditional name is RELATIVE CLAUSE; this name is so firmly established that you ought to know it. The same point emerges as for noun clauses: you can't recognise a relative clause just by looking at its signal word. For example, 'who had passed' in example (a) above could be either a noun clause or a relative clause, depending on the intended meaning. For present purposes it is not important to be able to classify subordinate clauses; the only thing that matters is to recognise their basic dependency relationships. This is just as well because noun clauses can be used in a way that makes them quite hard to distinguish from relative clauses, but either way their basic dependencies are the same. We shall look at some examples of this in the next unit.

EXERCISE ✎

Practising relative clauses

9.3

8. Here are some real-life examples (from a teenage magazine) of relative clauses. Without drawing complete diagrams for the whole sentence put square brackets round the relative clause and its signal word and underline the signal word (if there is one) and the noun that the relative clause depends on. Here is a worked example:

I like any <u>book</u> [<u>that</u> has pictures].

(a) 'I worship the ground she walks on,' says Ted, who had an affair with Liz Robins before he met Mary.
(b) Tim Barton spends every moment he can with wife Mary Smith.

(c) Many of the well-wishing calls are from singers who have carved out successful careers in the shadows of Sinatra's voice.

(d) One of the most persistent callers has been Shirley Farmer who wants to make it up with him before he dies.

(e) Frank feels she betrayed him in her autobiography by mentioning friends he had in the Mafia.

(f) From then on you will be LR UK's London correspondent covering every aspect of the show-business scene in Britain.

(g) Applications received after this date cannot be considered.

The third main use-based type of subordinate clause, after noun clauses and relative clauses, is the type that are used like adverbs (ADVERB CLAUSES).

Adverb clauses

✐ **EXERCISE**

Adverb clauses

9.4

9. What adverbs could be used to replace the subordinate clauses (without change of meaning) in the following examples?

(a) After that happened we all went home.

(b) Because that was so we had to take a bus.

(c) Although the situation was like that, we still had a good time.

(d) While that happened, we stayed inside.

(e) He came in making a lot of noise.

10. One of the characteristics of adverbs is that when they depend on a verb they can be used either before it or after it ('Quite often he sings in the bath'; 'He sings in the bath quite often'). Show that the same is true of adverb clauses using the examples above.

11. What changes of word order (without change of meaning) are possible for the following example? Do you think some of the orders are easier to understand than others? Pick the sentence with the most complicated order and draw a diagram for it.

I sleep well if I relax before I go to bed.

12. Prepare to complete the dependency analysis of the first part of the Pinker text (repeated below). The incomplete words are *as* and *for*, and you have to decide which word each of these words depend on. Be especially careful with *for* – follow the meaning, not the punctuation! (We shall discuss this example again in the next unit.)

> As you are reading these words, you are taking part in one
> . of the wonders of the natural world. For you and I belong to
> a species with a remarkable ability.

---

13. Some more real-life examples for you to practise on. Put square brackets round all the subordinate clauses (some of which are adverb clauses) and underline their signal words.

(a) In a startlingly frank article on homosexuality, the Vatican newspaper has urged Roman Catholics to respect gays, saying they can achieve sanctity in the Church if they abstain from sex.

(b) Moments after 10-year-old Charlotte Britton and her brother Charles, 8, had been playing on their lawn in Ripon, North Yorkshire, the flowerbeds and grass slid into a gaping crack which rapidly widened into a 30-foot-wide water-filled lagoon.

(c) When a politician is on song, as Mr Major was last week and Mr Blair was yesterday, the fashionable criticism of the campaign is revealed as the shallow stuff it often is.

(d) With no cameras in the courtroom to transform every objection and lawyer's huddle into a piece of live television drama, the Oklahoma City bombing trial has not created legal celebrities to match the glossy cast of the O. J. Simpson saga.

Most subordinate clauses fit into one of these three groups – noun, relative or adverb – but there are some that don't. This doesn't matter too much because the classification isn't part of your sentence analysis. What does matter is that you should see clearly how all the words fit together in the total network of dependencies. Table 9.1 gives a rough overview of the subordinate clauses that we have considered in the last two units. Clauses are classified vertically according to their structure (what signal-word, if any, do they have?) and horizontally according to their use, giving the three rough categories that we have introduced in this unit. I've filled a couple of cells with examples that go beyond those actually discussed.

Table 9.1

	Noun clause	Relative clause	Adverb clause
zero	I know [she left].	the girl [I met]	so cold [it snowed]
that	I know [*that* she left]	the girl [*that* I met]	so cold [*that* it snowed]
preposition	[*For* her to leave] is rude.	the girl [*for* you to meet]	snows [*if* it gets cold]
wh-pronoun	I wonder [*who* left]	the girl [*who* left]	snows [*whether* it's hot or cold]
non-finite	[*To* leave] would be rude.	the girl [*to* meet]	went [*to* meet her]

Sentence structures don't always leap out at you, and you may have to extract them bit by bit, a dependency here and a phrase there, until it all fits together. This can be complicated, and the secret of success (as in everything else in life) is to break the difficult problem down into smaller problems which are easier. To do this you may find it helpful to approach a sentence using the procedure shown below.

1 Classify the words that you feel fairly sure of.
2 Go through from left to right filling in the easiest dependencies between words that are next to each other, making sure that each of the dependencies is one of the patterns that we have found in this course. (If in doubt you can find them listed together in the index under 'Pattern'.)
3 Go through again adding any other dependencies that are now easier to see, but

   (a) make sure that none of the dependencies tangle, and
   (b) pay special attention to linking words (prepositions and coordinators) and other 'signal-words' for subordinate clauses. For each such word make sure you find its dependent (if it has one – it may not) and the word that it depends on.

4 If there are any coordinators (usually *and* or *or*), put in the coordination brackets – one curly pair for each coordinator, containing at least one pair of square brackets before each coordinator and one pair starting at the coordinator. If the coordination is complicated, number each coordinator and its curly brackets.
5 If you get stuck, try a 'top-down' approach, starting with the central dependencies. Look for the first finite verb, and ask whether there is any signal-word to its left that it could depend on. If not, draw a vertical arrow and take it as the sentence's head; then look for its dependents (subject, object, sharer, unclassified); and for each of these dependents, look

for its dependents and so on, building all the time on the arrows you've already drawn.

6 Check that every word has one arrow and that no arrows tangle (except as a result of coordination). You've finished!

EXERCISE ✎

Test your strength

9.5

14. The following example looks harmless, but it's surprisingly interesting! Try it. As always, you'll make your job much easier if you arrange the line-breaks so that the minimum of dependency arrows cross from one line to the next; so think before you copy the example out.

However, if the intersection you are about to enter has a light which is going to change soon, traffic from behind may be storming up at a breakneck pace.

MODEL TEXT

The analysis is complete now that we know (from question 12) that *as* and *for* both depend on *are*. In case you haven't already found it, the complete analysis is shown in Appendix I.

SUMMARY

- Subordinate clauses are traditionally classified in terms of basic word-classes: noun clauses and adverb clauses are used roughly like nouns and adverbs, while relative clauses are used somewhat like adjectives. These classes are helpful in thinking about grammatical patterns, but they won't appear as such in your analyses.

- The classification of subordinate clauses according to use cuts right across the classification according to their signal-word, which is a matter of structure. This can be seen clearly in Table 9.1.

- If a sentence's structure is hard to see, it becomes easier if you break the problem down into smaller ones by applying the system laid out on p. 83.

1. Give a complete analysis of the following:

To open the older-style manual doors from inside,

you need to pull down the window and reach outside.

Keep well away from the doors while the train is travelling,

and if you have to stand, make sure

you hold on firmly to a strap or hand-rail.

---

2. Update your 100-word text (which should be more or less perfect by now!)

10

SENTENCES AND INFORMATION: *IT, THERE,* APPOSITION AND PUNCTUATION

We've now dealt with all the main syntactic patterns of English – coordination and various different subordination patterns in which one word can depend on another. However, we must also recognise the fact that there are numerous other minor patterns, including three which it would be irresponsible to ignore because they are so common. In fact, by a strange chance all three are illustrated in the last sentence: 'the fact that . . .', 'there are . . .' and 'it would be . . .'. By another happy coincidence all three have something to do with the way in which we distribute information among the words in a sentence, so we shall take this as a general theme for the unit.

EXERCISE ✎

Apposition

10.1

1. The following sentences from a newspaper report each contain two noun expansions which both refer to the same person or thing. Put square brackets round these noun expansions.

  (a) Margery Manners, one of Britain's best-loved music hall and variety performers, died of cancer in a London hospital yesterday, aged 71.
  (b) Mrs Manners, whose career spanned more than 50 years, was best known for her signature tune 'Bring me the sunshine of your smile', which sold more than a million copies.

2. Each of the following pairs of sentences could be collapsed into a single sentence, without subordinate clauses, which gives the same information. What are these sentences?

(a) Bill Clinton is the President of the USA.
 Bill Clinton is the world's most powerful person.
(b) My friend is coming to supper tonight.
 This friend of mine is called Fred.
(c) That idiot has left the door open again.
 That idiot is Pat.
(d) A village nestles among the elm trees at the foot of the hill.
 This village is Skenfrith.
(e) Global temperatures are rising steadily.
 This is a matter of great concern to us all.

---

3. A 'determiner', you recall (Unit 4), is a pronoun that can combine with a common noun. Here are two examples:

this book, you students

How are the meanings of the pronoun and the common noun related to each other?

---

4. You need to know how to diagram examples like 'my friend Pat'. Let's assume we have to link the two parts, 'my friend' and 'Pat', by a dependency; which part depends on the other? Why? (Use evidence from the earlier exercises.)

These questions introduced you to an important and very common syntactic pattern, in which two words offer different ways of defining the same person or thing. In simple cases both words are nouns and they are simply put next to each other, separated only by their own dependents (e.g. 'my friend Fred') but in other cases they are separated by an obligatory preposition *of* ('the village of Skenfrith') and in others again the first word is not a noun ('. . . are rising, a matter . . .'). This pattern has a traditional name which you should know: APPOSITION. So far as there is any evidence, it supports a dependency analysis in which the second word depends on the first, as shown in Figure 10.1.

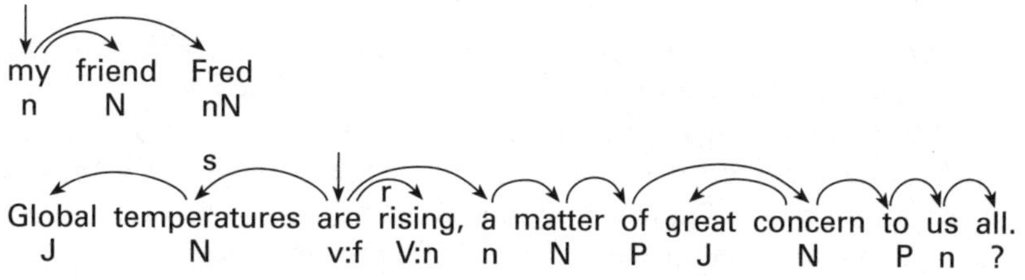

Apposition

Figure 10.1

Noun clauses in apposition to nouns

10.2

5. The second part of an apposition can be a noun clause. Find examples in the following sentences, and draw a diagram for the first one.

(a) The fact that it rained is irrelevant.
(b) I'm gobsmacked at the idea that you're getting married.
(c) Your discovery that the universe is made of nouns is quite interesting.
(d) I suddenly had the idea of turning all the arrows round.

6. Why do we bother to put a noun clause into apposition with an ordinary noun? Does it make the syntax simpler (fewer arrows, labels, etc.), or more flexible? Use the following examples (which aren't all grammatical) as evidence.

(a) I got the idea that someone was following me.
(b) I got that someone was following me.
(c) We talked about the claim that he'd cheated.
(d) We talked about that he'd cheated.
(e) The awful thought that we might never get out came to my mind.
(f) Awful that we might never get out came to my mind.
(g) Did the fact that it cost so much influence your decision?
(h) Did that it cost so much influence your decision?

7. Find at least five different ways of 'packaging' the information in the following sentences into a single sentence, and pick the one you like best.

(a) There are no exams this term.
(b) It's true.
(c) It's wonderful.
(d) We're making the most of it.

To summarise, one way to make a noun clause more user-friendly is to put it in apposition with an ordinary noun, which allows the best of two worlds: the full range of syntactic possibilities for a noun, combined with those for a verb. Figure 10.2 shows the structure of a typical example. As we shall now see, another way to increase user-friendliness is to postpone the noun clause till the end of the sentence.

Figure 10.2

10.3

8. The following sentences express the same meaning. What differences do you find in their syntactic structures, and how can you generalise the difference? (I.e. when is such a difference possible?)

    (a) That you remembered my birthday is nice.
    (b) It is nice that you remembered my birthday.

---

9. Which word does the subordinate clause depend on in (b) (question 8)? Why? (Use your judgement on the grammaticality of the next sentences as evidence.) Draw diagrams for both examples in question 8.

    (a) The fact that it is nice that you remembered my birth-
         day matters greatly.
    (b) The fact that it is nice matters greatly that you remem-
         bered my birthday.

---

10. The examples discussed so far have all involved noun clauses, but relative clauses can be delayed in similar ways. Suggest a diagram for the next sentence. (Don't worry about the fact that the relative clause can't occur earlier in the sentence.)

    It was you that I was looking for.

---

11. Using the pattern in question 10, find at least five ways of rephrasing the following sentence, and decide what difference these rephrasings make to the sentence's meaning.

    Pat wrote that essay for Jo on her PC last night.

---

12. Some real-life examples from Greenbaum (1996:174). Pick out the subordinate clauses that have been delayed.

    (a) It's a shame he's not going to be back here.
    (b) It is physically impossible to force myself to work
         sometimes.
    (c) It's the young miner I feel sorry for, especially one with
         a young family.

(d) It is what you put in and what you achieve which counts.

(e) It wasn't till I was perhaps twenty-five or thirty that I read them and enjoyed them.

The examples in questions 8–12 illustrate a very common pattern in English, in which the pronoun *it* allows a subordinate clause to be delayed until later in the sentence, thereby making the clause easier for a reader or listener to handle. (In a more advanced course in grammar we could go into the reasons why this is so.) Figure 10.3 illustrates this pattern for both noun clauses and relative clauses.

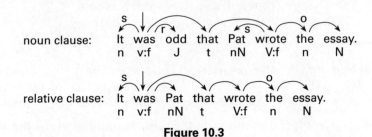

Figure 10.3

What all these patterns have in common is that they allow us, as speakers and writers, to control the rate of 'information-flow' in a sentence. Apposition speeds it up by collapsing two clauses into one (e.g. 'I met my friend Pat' collapses 'I met my friend' and 'My friend is Pat'), whereas the use of delaying *it* slows it down by allowing a subordinate clause to be delayed until later in the sentence. Both of these strategies are important and useful on different occasions in writing and speaking as ways of helping the reader or listener. There is a third strategy, illustrated by this very sentence: the use of delaying *there*.

EXERCISE ✎

Delaying there

10.4

13. What is the subject of the sentence 'There is a third strategy'? Why? Why is there some uncertainty? What is the word-class of *there*? Is this *there* the same as the one in 'I met her there'?

---

14. Which word does *a* depend on in 'There is a third strategy'? Draw a diagram for the sentence.

---

15. Some more real-life examples from Greenbaum (1996:177). In each case underline the delaying *there* and put in square brackets the noun expansion which has been delayed.

    (a) When I went through Romania there were guards there as well.

    (b) Are there any particular events that you can remember about your father?

    (c) There should be quite a few people coming tomorrow.

Delaying *it* and *there* are just two of the strategies that English grammar offers us for adjusting the flow of information inside a sentence. There are several others which we can't explore properly here, but which are worth mentioning however briefly. Here is a list of variations on a single theme, the meaning expressed by the first sentence:

    (a) They gave a photograph which had been signed by Elvis to Pat.

    (b) They gave to Pat a photograph which had been signed by Elvis.

    (c) They gave Pat a photograph which had been signed by Elvis.

    (d) They gave a photograph to Pat which had been signed by Elvis.

    (e) A photograph which had been signed by Elvis was given to Pat.

    (f) Pat was given a photograph which had been signed by Elvis.

Each of these sentences presents the same information, but organises it differently. Any efficient language user should be aware of the range of options available for organising information within a sentence.

    Our final question is a profound one: what is a sentence, and what does it have to do with the organisation of information? In more practical terms, how do we know when to use a full stop (or whatever you call '.')?

✐ **EXERCISE**

10.5

Sentence boundaries

16. (Don't worry if you did exercises like this at school!) Here is a short passage which I have un-punctuated. Please punctuate it.

> you know the feeling you meet someone for the first time and it's as if you've known each other all your lives everything goes smoothly you see exactly what she means she sees exactly what you mean you laugh at the same things what you both say has a perfect rhythm you feel wonderful about the meeting you're doing everything right and you think she's terrific too but you know the other kind of encounter too you meet someone you try to get along with them to make a good impression but nothing goes right

17. Diagram the words in this passage up to *smoothly* and work out a simple rule for using punctuation when you already know the syntactic structure. Make sure that your rule explains what's wrong with the following attempt at punctuation:

> You know, the feeling you meet. Someone for the first time and it's as if you've known each other. All your lives everything goes smoothly.

---

18. The model answer to question 16 shows where the punctuation marks were, but nothing more. Try to guess which actual punctuation marks the author used at those points. What do you think of her decisions (given in the model answer to the present question)? What further punctuation rules are needed to supplement the one you built in question 17?

These exercises should have convinced you that 'sentence' is a rather unsatisfactory technical term. If we define it in terms of grammatical structures, as a group of words held together by dependency or coordination, then punctuation is only a poor guide; but if we take punctuation as the basis, there will be numerous examples where the grammatical structure disagrees. It doesn't really matter so long as the notion 'sentence' is in the background, as it is has been throughout this book. But we have all been brought up with the idea that punctuation and grammar are in step, which raises questions about 'sentences' like the one you are reading now, with its initial *But*. Similarly, even our short extract from Pinker contained a 'sentence' starting with *For* which actually depends syntactically on the verb of the preceding 'sentence'. As our model dependency analysis of this text shows, syntactic structure can transcend punctuation.

SUMMARY

- 'Apposition' is the relationship between two words (or word expansions) that refer to the same person or thing – e.g. 'my friend Pat', 'the village of Chubley', 'the fact that it was raining', 'It rained, something unusual for this time of year.'
- In apposition, the second word depends on the first.
- The use of delaying *it* or *there* allows various sentence patterns containing a subordinate clause or phrase after the head verb, as in 'There was a bang', 'It is odd that it rained', 'It was Pat that broke it.'
- The use of apposition and of delaying *it* and *there* are some of the strategies that English offers for controlling the flow of information by either speeding it up or slowing it down.
- Punctuation signals both syntactic structure (dependency and coordination) and also information structure. These two

requirements often conflict, so it is perhaps just as well that we don't need to define the notion 'sentence'.

Something rather different, which should be fun!

1. Punctuate (and capitalise) the following love letter:

> Dear John I want a man who knows what love is all about you are generous kind thoughtful people who are not like you admit to being useless and inferior you have ruined me for other men I yearn for you I have no feelings whatsoever when we're apart I can be forever happy will you let me be yours Gloria

2. Now do it again but this time assume that Gloria hates John.

> Dear John I want a man who knows what love is all about you are generous kind thoughtful people who are not like you admit to being useless and inferior you have ruined me for other men I yearn for you I have no feelings whatsoever when we're apart I can be forever happy will you let me be yours Gloria

3. Do a grammatical analysis of the first couple of lines to illustrate the different structures in your two texts.

APPENDIX I: MODEL ANALYSIS OF A 100-WORD TEXT

From Steven Pinker, *The Language Instinct* (1994: 15)

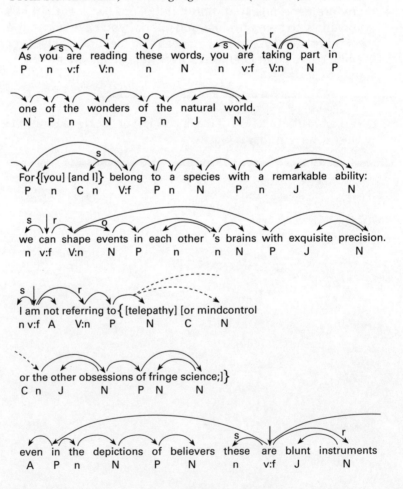

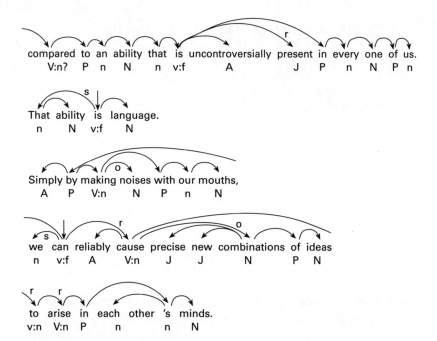

compared to an ability that is uncontroversially present in every one of us.
V:n? P n N n v:f A J P n N P n

That ability is language.
n N v:f N

Simply by making noises with our mouths,
A P V:n N P n N

we can reliably cause precise new combinations of ideas
n v:f A V:n J J N P N

to arise in each other 's minds.
v:n V:n P n n N

APPENDIX II: APPROACHES TO GRAMMAR

You might like to know how the approach that we have taken in this course compares with other ways of studying English grammar. What other approaches are there, and why have I chosen this approach rather than the alternatives?

TRADITIONAL GRAMMAR

This course is part of a long tradition of grammatical analysis which stretches back two thousand years to the grammarians of Ancient Greece and Rome. They were describing the structures of Greek and Latin (not English, of course!), where they discovered all the basic ideas of grammar – word-classes, dependency links, coordination, dependent types (such as subjects and objects) and form-based contrasts like finiteness. They worked through Greek and Latin in loving detail, producing a body of terminology and ideas that have been handed down, more or less intact, to the present day. This is so-called 'traditional grammar', which you will find alive and well in most modern books that deal with grammar, especially dictionaries and grammars of foreign languages. It is also the foundation on which all modern thinking about grammar rests.

Nearly all the ideas and terms used in this course are traditional; the exceptions are:

- the word-class 'determiner' (which later disappears) and the dependent label 'sharer';
- the assumptions about the direction of dependency in some patterns (especially around auxiliary verbs, determiners and prepositions);
- some points where traditional classification is simply wrong (as it is when it treats both *this* and *joke* as adjectives in 'this joke book');
- the diagramming system, which is brand new.

Otherwise anyone familiar with traditional grammar already knows most of what is in this book. In particular, they know that words are the only 'real' units of grammar (in contrast with the approaches mentioned below where word groups are important).

Traditional grammar is sometimes taught in schools. At one time it was so widely taught that some British schools were called 'grammar schools', and in the late nineteenth century sentence diagramming became very popular throughout Europe and America. Even today there are schools which teach children how to do it. However, grammar teaching has been generally abandoned in many parts of the English-speaking world during the last few decades. The objection to teaching traditional grammar wasn't so much that the grammatical analyses were wrong but rather that teaching it was a waste of time. There was no research evidence that it helped students to write better English, and teachers did not see any other benefits of learning grammatical analysis (such as in teaching foreign languages or general mind-training). Furthermore, the method of teaching was often very unsatisfactory as teachers were often dogmatic and ignorant, and grammar was always 'prescriptive' because by definition Standard English forms were grammatical and non-standard forms were ungrammatical. In retrospect the death of grammar-teaching may not have been such a bad thing, but many people believe it is time for a revival.

Compared with traditional school grammar this course has four main distinctive features.

1 The pedagogical approach is 'discovery learning', which is the opposite of dogma: students discover the grammar for themselves, and in so doing they learn the factual basis for the analysis.

2 The grammar is descriptive rather than prescriptive, so non-standard English defines its own 'grammatical' and 'ungrammatical' forms.

3 I have kept terminology to the absolute minimum. (I hope you noticed this, and appreciated it!) In school grammar, terminology was an end in itself rather than a tool, which is how I view it.

4 The new diagramming system taught in this book is better than the rather small number of systems used in teaching traditional grammar in school. On the one hand, it gives more information (especially about the order of words) and, on the other, it is more practical because it can be written directly on the text being analysed.

In the last few decades there has been an explosion of interest in the theory of grammar, which is part of the modern subject called 'linguistics'. The new ideas have combined with the practical need for good reference grammars of English (for the benefit of foreign language learners) to produce a body of new work which we can call 'modern descriptive grammar'. Any academic bookshop will have a collection of formidable volumes called *A Grammar of Modern English* (or some such title). These grammars use the ideas and terminology of traditional grammar (with just a few specific changes, such as the introduction of 'determiner' and various other terms such as 'adjunct' and 'disjunct'). But unlike traditional grammar they avoid prescription, they cover casual spoken English as well as written English, and they use a framework of general ideas about the nature of sentence structure that comes from recent theorising in linguistics.

You could see this course as an elementary introduction to this kind of grammar, but there is still one distinctive characteristic here. In most modern descriptive work the grammar is organised around notions like 'noun phrase' and 'verb phrase', which we have called simply 'noun expansions' and 'verb expansions'. The difference isn't just a matter of terminology, but reflects a fundamentally different view of the nature of sentence structure. The approach we have followed in this course is the traditional one: sentence structure is a network of relationships (dependencies) between individual words. Once all these relationships have been described, the job is done. In contrast, modern descriptive grammars tend to take 'phrase structure' as basic, where 'phrase' is used very generally to cover any kind of word expansion (or even potential expansion) including clauses and sentences. In this view, the grammarian's job is to find the phrases, even when they consist of just a single word.

To make the difference concrete, where we have recognised a single noun as the subject of a verb, modern grammars generally recognise a noun phrase as the subject of a whole clause. For example, in 'Small babies cry' we say that *babies* is the subject of *cry*, where they say that 'small babies' is the subject of 'small babies cry'. This can make analysis very much more complicated; for example, a simple two-word sentence like 'Babies cry' has to be given a phrase structure in which *babies* counts twice, once as a word and then as a phrase. For a descriptive grammar such extra phrases are generally not much help, and I think we have been better off without them during this course.

TRANSFORMATIONAL GRAMMAR

The most influential theory about sentence structure is actually a series of sub-theories which we can call, collectively, 'transformational grammar'. It is the brain-child of the most famous linguist of the century, Noam Chomsky (of the Massachussetts Institute of Technology). The notion of phrase structure is fundamental to Chomsky's theory, so if his theory is right, it should be impossible to do without phrases. If you take the study of grammar to a higher level you will probably have to make up your mind about the pros and cons of these two positions. Neither side is obviously right or obviously wrong, so it may take you some time to decide.

One of Chomsky's main ideas is that some of the complexities of grammar are best explained if we give a sentence a rather abstract structure which is only indirectly related to the actual words. The rules that relate the two are called 'transformations', so the whole approach can also be called 'transformational grammar'. This view of sentence structure may or may not be right, but it has certainly stimulated a vast amount of very high-quality theorising. Because of this emphasis on theory, books on transformational grammar tend to offer depth rather than breadth. This is the reverse of the approach I have taken here: I have tried to give you a broad view of most of English grammar, rather than a deep understanding of any part. But this is just a pedagogical decision rather than a matter of theory or principle.

SYSTEMIC FUNCTIONAL GRAMMAR

This is a very different theory of grammar, invented by Michael Halliday (of the Universities of London and Sydney), which has had considerable influence on school grammar. You should know that this is the first major theory that I myself learned to use, and its influence shows in this course. Unlike Chomsky, Halliday does aim at breadth of coverage, and he also aims at very concrete analyses which are tied closely to the actual words. Both of these characteristics are true of this course, and are ultimately due to Halliday's influence; and once again most of what you have learned in this course would be a good basis for a more theoretical course in his theory.

Three things distinguish this course from one in systemic functional grammar, all of which have been mentioned above: the emphasis on dependencies between words rather than word-groups, the diagramming system, and the reduced terminology.

WORD GRAMMAR

This is my own pet theory, which I must just mention in order to make it clear that this course doesn't exist in a theoretical vacuum. I have deliberately avoided theoretical issues because I don't think that is what an absolute beginner needs. I have tried to avoid theoretical tub-thumping or agonising, and have kept as far as possible to the common ground. On the other hand, if challenged I would defend virtually everything in this course as theoretically sound.

The main distinctive characteristics of word grammar are its use of dependencies rather than phrase structure, and its concreteness, so it's no coincidence that these are both also characteristics of this course. If you should, by any chance, learn more about word grammar, you will find that it offers solutions to all the theoretical problems that we noticed on the way, as well as providing a general theoretical framework for the details that we have covered.

MODEL ANSWERS

UNIT 1
WORD-CLASSES

1.2 3–4. A meaning-based explanation doesn't work. One based on word-classes does. If a sentence consists of a noun and a verb as in question 1, the noun must come before the verb. If a three-word sentence starts with a noun and finishes with a noun, the word between them must be a verb.

1.3 5. (a) False. (b) Contradictory. *(c), *(d). Both ungrammatical.

1.4 6. Pick . . . nouns . . . verbs . . . sentences.
　　　V　　N　　　N　　　　N

Children may know . . . word . . . find . . . pronounce.
N　v　V　　　N　　　V　　　V

　　7. times (e.g. He times himself when running.)
sounds (That sounds fishy.)
ring (He bought a ring.)
round (He'll round the bend soon. It's round. He bought a round of drinks.)
resort (We never resort to cheating.)

1.5 8. Every sentence needs a verb.
　　9. A word just before or after *annoys* or *knows* may be a noun but not a verb.
　10. A noun has just two forms, a singular and plural (e.g. *idea, ideas*). A verb usually has at least four forms, e.g. *think, thinks, thought, thinking; know, knows, knew, knowing.*

Table A1.1

V	think	thinks	thought	thinking
N	idea	ideas		
N	thought	thoughts		
V	get	gets	got	getting
V	know	knows	knew	knowing
V	grow	grows	grew	growing
V	flash	flashes	flashed	flashing
N	flash	flashes		
N	word	words		
V	say	says	said	saying
N	saying	sayings		

1.6 11. e.g. loathe, think, feel, run, eat – in fact, virtually every verb allows this pattern.

12. agree-ment (excitement, amusement, movement . . .), explor-ation (derivation, explanation, examination . . .), jump (sleep, walk, run . . .), refus-al (removal, arrival, denial . . .).

13. *-ment*, *-ation* and *-al* are only added to words borrowed from French or Latin.

1.7 14. *students* (b), (c), *verbs* (e), *Sian* (g). *Sian* or Sian in (h), according to meaning.

15. *house, children, good, lightning, say, will, do, House.*

2.1 1. 12 (4 x 3)

2. . . . (an) M2 that has something to do with M1.

2.2 3.

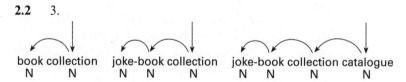

book collection   joke-book collection   joke-book collection catalogue
N   N   N   N   N   N   N   N   N

Figure A.1

4.

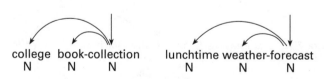

college book-collection   lunchtime weather-forecast
N   N   N   N   N   N

Figure A.2

5.

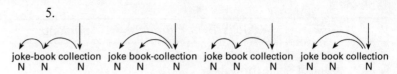

joke-book collection   joke book-collection   joke book collection   joke book collection
N   N   N   N   N   N   N   N   N   N   N   N

Figure A.3

2.3   6.   *good* can be used after *is* and *very* but not after *the*; vice versa for *joke*.

7.   apple,   big,   extreme,   grammatical,   grammaticality, hateful,

    N   J   J   J   N   J

life, lifelike, likeable, likely, linguistic, linguistics, possible,

    N   J   J   J   J   N   J

possibility, pretty, size

    N   J   N

8.   *Nice* depends on *house*, not on *little*, because (unlike *very*) it can depend on *house* without *little*, and it cannot depend on *little* without *house*.

2.4   9.

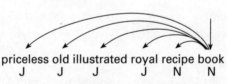

priceless old illustrated royal recipe book
J   J   J   J   N   N

Figure A.4

10.   There's some freedom to change the order of pre-dependents – maybe you could reverse the order of *illustrated* and *royal*, and maybe the first three words could have been in a different order. But it's impossible to put *recipe* earlier: *'recipe royal book', etc. because adjectives have to precede nouns.

11.

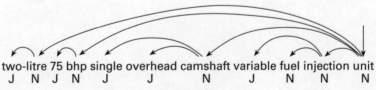

two-litre 75 bhp single overhead camshaft variable fuel injection unit
J N J N   J   J   N   J   N   N

Figure A.5

All adjectives and nouns that depend on the same noun do follow the rule, in spite of the apparent jumble of adjectives and nouns in the analysis. Where adjectives follow nouns, they depend on different words.

12.   A unit for variable injection of fuel with a single overhead camshaft with/of 75 bhp of two litres.

2.5   13.   Because *English* would have to depend on *joke*, but this is impossible because words have to be as close as possible to the word they depend on. You might think the rule is just that a word has to be next to the word it depends on, but that can't be right – just think of 'old French houses'. The easiest way to express the rule is simply to ban the crossing of arrows; this explains the badness of all the examples.

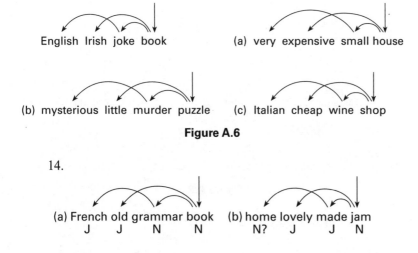

English Irish joke book   (a) very expensive small house

(b) mysterious little murder puzzle   (c) Italian cheap wine shop

Figure A.6

14.

(a) French old grammar book   (b) home lovely made jam
      J   J   N   N   N?   J   J   N

(c) historical old linguistics book
      J   J   N   N

Figure A.7

All are * because dependency arrows cross each other.

3.1   1.   From Greenbaum (1996: 159–60).

UNIT 3
LINKING WORDS

aboard, about, above, across, after, against, along, amid(st), among(st), anti, apropos, around, as, at, atop, bar, before, behind, below, beneath, beside(s), between, beyond, but, circa, concerning, considering, cum, despite, down, during, except, excepting, excluding, failing, following, for, from, given, in, including, inside, into, less, like, minus, near, nearby, next, notwithstanding, of, off, on, onto, out, outside, over, past, pending, per, plus, post, pro, qua, re, regarding, round, save, since, than, through, throughout, till, times, to, toward(s), under, unlike, until, unto, upon, versus, via, vis-à-vis, with, within, without, worth.

Greenbaum also gives a list of about eighty complex prepositions on pp. 161–2.

3.2   2.   The heads have meanings that are predictable, so they're not at all important. The important words are the dependents.

3.   *Behind* must be the head, because 'behind Pat' means a place.

3.3   4.   (b), (e) and (f) are *; (d) is a little strange, but it improves if you lengthen the second preposition-expansion: 'book with small print of bad jokes about linguists and frogs'.

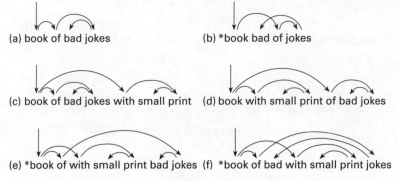

(a) book of bad jokes

(b) *book bad of jokes

(c) book of bad jokes with small print

(d) book with small print of bad jokes

(e) *book of with small print bad jokes

(f) *book of bad with small print jokes

Figure A.8

Look at Figure 3.1 on p. 24.

According to my analysis 1, all the bad ones have tangled dependencies, but example (b) should be OK according to analysis 3, and example (e) according to analysis 2. Analysis 4 makes the same distinctions as mine does, but is much more complicated.

5.   (a) and (c) are *, as expected; in (d) and (e) the dependent noun is earlier in the sentence: *who* and *person*.

3.4   6.   No limit.

7.

(a) students of linguistics with long hair

(b) books of jokes about linguists with long hair

(c) books of jokes about linguists with weak punchlines

(d) books of jokes about linguists with red covers

Figure A.9

3.5   8.   Yes to all questions. A suitable example would be 'books and journals with shelf-marks and accession numbers and without covers and binding'. You did well if you thought of one!

9.   Yes to all questions. For coordinated adjective and noun think of examples like 'private and business addresses' or 'educational and research activities'.

3.6   10.

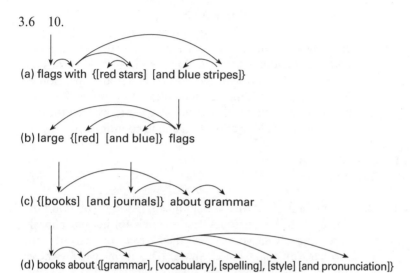

(a) flags with {[red stars] [and blue stripes]}

(b) large {[red] [and blue]} flags

(c) {[books] [and journals]} about grammar

(d) books about {[grammar], [vocabulary], [spelling], [style] [and pronunciation]}

Figure A.10

11.

(a) $\{_1[\{[_2\text{red}] [\text{white}] [\text{and}_2 \text{blue}]\}_2] [\text{or}_1 \text{pink}]\}_1$
$\{[_1\text{red}] [\text{white}] [\text{and}_1\{[_2\text{blue}] [\text{or}_2 \text{pink}]\}_2]\}_1$

(b) $\{[_1\{[_2\text{red}] [\text{or}_2 \text{white}]\}_2], [\text{blue}], [\text{pink}] [\text{or}_1 \text{gold}]\}_1$
$\{_1[\text{red}] [\text{or}_1\{[\text{white}], [\text{blue}], [\text{pink}] [\text{or}_2 \text{gold}]\}_2]\}_1$

(c) $\{_1[\text{red}] [\text{and}_1\{_2[\text{white}] [\text{or}_2\{_3[\text{blue}] [\text{and}_3 \text{pink}]\}_3]\}_2]\}_1$
$\{_1[\text{red}] [\text{and}_1\{_2[\{_3[\text{white}] [\text{or}_3 \text{blue}]\}_3[\text{and}_2 \text{pink}]\}_2]\}_1$
$\{_1[\{_2[\text{red}] [\text{and}_2 \text{white}]\}_2] [\text{or}_1\{_3[\text{blue}] [\text{and}_3 \text{pink}]\}_3]\}_1$
$\{_1[\{_2[\text{red}] [\text{and}_2\{[_3\text{white}] [\text{or}_3 \text{blue}]\}_3]\}_2] [\text{and}_1 \text{pink}]\}_1$
$\{_1[\{_2[\{_3[\text{red}] [\text{and}_3 \text{white}]\}_3] [\text{or}_2 \text{blue}]\}_2] [\text{and}_1 \text{pink}]\}_1$

Figure A.11

12.

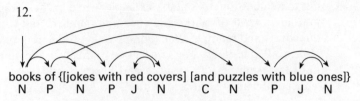

books of {[jokes with red covers] [and puzzles with blue ones]}
N   P   N   P   J   N   C   N   P   J   N

Figure A.12

The example is tricky for two reasons. It is completely grammatical, and yet arrows tangle, and the words inside each pair of square brackets don't make a single expansion: for example, 'jokes with red covers' is not an expansion of *jokes*. The diagramming system allows us to show this complication without problems, but we need to weaken the No-tangling Principle to allow tangling in coordination.

**UNIT 4
SUB-
CLASSIFICATION**

4.1   1. No.
         2. N1.

4.2   3. (a) her, him, it, us, them, one (it exists even if you don't use it!) (b) hers, his, its, ours, theirs, one's (c) herself, himself, itself, ourselves, yourselves, themselves, oneself (d) one another (e) that, these, those (f) which, what, whose; (maybe) where, when, why, how (g) whoever, etc. (h) some, neither, either, any, each.

         4. (a) The adjective follows the noun. (b) Only one. (c) No. (d) someone, somebody, something, somewhere; no-one, nobody, nothing, nowhere; everyone, everybody, everything, everywhere; anyone, anybody, anything, anywhere; sometime, never, always, ever (?).

4.3   5. *British* is an adjective, and *Bishop, Frenchman, Latin, Mathematics,* and *Member* (of Parliament) are common nouns. Somewhat surprisingly, *midnight* and *today* are both proper nouns.

4.4   6. (a) you, us (b) his, its, one's (e) that, those (f) which, what, whose (g) whichever, whatever (h) some, neither, either, any, each.

         7. (b) her/hers, our/ours, their/theirs (h) no/none.

4.5   8. 'book' can be omitted, but 'this' can't. The same is true for any pronoun combined with a singular countable common noun.

         9. No.

4.6 10.

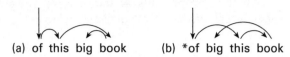

(a) of this big book   (b) *of big this book

Figure A.13

The No-tangling Principle bans the tangling of the arrows in the second example.

4.7 11. A pronoun.

12. *'s.*

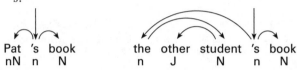

Pat 's book   the other student 's book
nN n   N   n   J   N   n   N

Figure A.14

13. Because *'s* is separated from the head noun and follows the whole of its expansion.

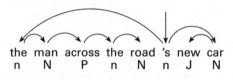

the man across the road 's new car
n   N   P   n   N   n   J   N

Figure A.15

5.1 1. *cry.*

2. e.g. small babies, babies without hair; people cry, people cry lots, little boys never cry. Expansions of *cry.*

5.2 3. (a) Pat. (b) Jo. (c) Because of the word order. The giver of the kiss is before the verb, and the receiver after it.

4. *adores beer Charlie; *adores Charlie beer; *beer adores Charlie; Beer Charlie adores (OK, in special contexts, e.g. before 'but wine he can't stand'); Charlie adores beer (normal); *Charlie beer adores. Because the adorer (the person who has the feeling) is immediately before the verb and the object of adoration is normally after it, or (exceptionally) before the adorer.

5. (Meaning:) The feeler and stimulus of *adores* are (expressed by) its subject and object, but vice versa for *attracts.* (Word order:) A verb's subject is immediately before it, and its object is normally after it but may be before its subject.

6. *He* and *she* can only be used as subjects, and *him* and *her* only as objects. *I – me, we – us, they – them.*

7. If the subject is singular, the verb has the ending *-s*, but not if

**UNIT 5
VERB
EXPANSIONS**

it is plural; the plurality of the object is irrelevant. Only present-tense verbs. (We shall discuss tense in the next unit.)

5.3   8.

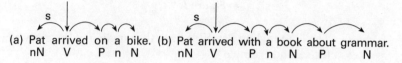

(a) Pat arrived on a bike.
    nN   V   P n N

(b) Pat arrived with a book about grammar.
    nN   V   P n N P   N

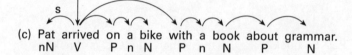

(c) Pat arrived on a bike with a book about grammar.
    nN   V   P n N P n N P   N

(d) Pat arrived on a bike with red mudguards.
    nN   V   P n N P J   N

Figure A.16

9.

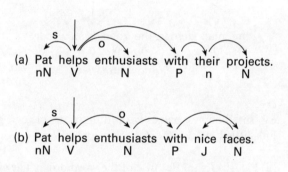

(a) Pat helps enthusiasts with their projects.
    nN V   N   P n   N

(b) Pat helps enthusiasts with nice faces.
    nN V   N   P J N

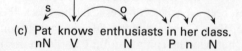

(c) Pat knows enthusiasts in her class.
    nN V   N   P n N

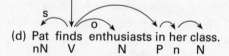

(d) Pat finds enthusiasts in her class.
    nN V   N   P n N

Figure A.17

10.   (a) and (d), because a preposition cannot depend on a following noun. If a preposition depends on a verb that also has an object, the object normally comes first but can follow the preposition expansion if the latter is long.

11.

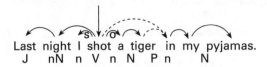

Last night I shot a tiger in my pyjamas.
J   nN n V n N P n   N

Figure A.18

12. A preposition can't depend on a following noun, nor can a preposition that depends on a verb separate the verb from its subject. (The second rule is an oversimplification, but it applies in the present case.)

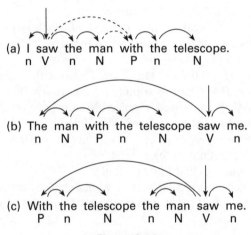

(a) I saw the man with the telescope.
    n V n   N   with n   N

(b) The man with the telescope saw me.
    n   N   P n   N   V n

(c) With the telescope the man saw me.
    P n   N   n   N V n

Figure A.19

5.4 13. The second exchange is normal because 'a good friend' is a characteristic of Pat, i.e. she is an example of a good friend. The first exchange is odd because Pat and the good friend are different people linked only by the 'having', so without the verb there is no relationship. Like *has*: knows, wants; like *is*: became, seems.

14. is, became, seems. Yes, they are the verbs that treat the following dependent semantically as a quality of the subject; adjectives define qualities, so they are allowed. But the other verbs need to link the subject to a different person (or thing), so an adjective won't do. The same is true of other adjectives.

5.5 15. (a), (b), (d), (g), (h), (j).

16. (a), (d), (e), (f?).

5.6 17. (a) *quickly = quick + ly* (b) common noun (c) sharer (d) verb (e) probably not.

18. 1, 2, 4.

19. For example: recently, immediately, strangely, spontaneously, frequently, often, once, sometimes, now, then.

20.   adjective or adverb.

UNIT 6
VERB
CHAINS

6.1   1.   *reading* depends on *are*, because *reading* can be omitted but *are* can't. Importance is irrelevant, and so is the fact that the second verb is 'understood' when omitted.

2.   Sharer ('r'), because *are* and *reading* share their subject *you* in just the same way as *are* and *happy*: 'reading' and 'happy' are both characteristics of 'you'.

3.   Yes.

6.2   4.   (a), (b) *were*; (c) *being*; (d) *be*; (e) *been*

5.   No. First verbs are always either present tense or past tense forms, but second verbs never are.

6.   The first, because this is the verb of which *you* and *she* is the subject. *Can* doesn't vary when the subject changes.

6.3   7.   They're not present-tense forms because their meaning is different (they express commands etc. rather than statements) and they don't need a subject. Moreover *be* is imperative but not a present-tense form. They must be finite because they can be the only verb in a sentence (which must contain at least one finite verb).

8.   (a) finite (b) non-finite (c) finite.

9.   Replace the regular verb (e.g. *analysed*) by an irregular one which has distinct forms for past tense and non-finite (e.g. *did – done*).

6.4   10.   We add *not* or *n't* to an auxiliary verb, but not to a full verb.

11.   An auxiliary verb. It's used in the absence of any other auxiliary verb because it has no meaning.

12.   Shakespeare added *not* to any kind of verb.

13.   We reverse the normal order of a finite auxiliary verb and its subject. In the absence of any other auxiliary verb, we use DO, which is an auxiliary verb but has no meaning.

14.   He reversed the normal order of any finite verb and its subject.

6.5   15.   For me: are, can, could, did, do, had, have, may, might, ought (to), shall, should, used (to), were, will, would. Certainly not: begin (to), tended (to), want (to).

16.   am/'m, are/'re, had/'d, has/'s, have/'ve, is/'s, shall/'ll, will/'ll. They are all auxiliary verbs. There is a short form just in pronunciation for: could, do, should, would.

17.   Three: *he*, *'s* and *working*, because *he* and *'s* need to be classified separately as pronoun and verb – otherwise the sentence has no verb.

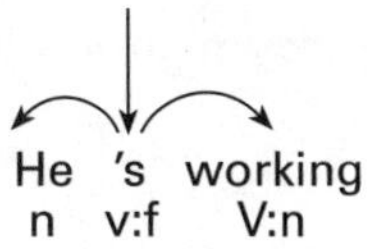

He 's working
n v:f V:n

Figure A.20

18. For me, (a), (e) and (f) are normal, but not (b), (c) or (d); so possessive HAVE is not an auxiliary verb for me.

6.6 19. No.
20. No.

UNIT 7 FANCY VERB CHAINS

7.1 1. Before a non-finite verb of any kind.
2. A verb. *try* → *to* → *get*.

7.2 3. The grammar allows 'to promise' to be repeated any number of times. For example:

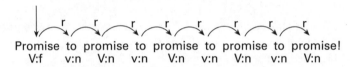

r r r r r r r r
Promise to promise to promise to promise to promise!
V:f v:n V:n v:n V:n v:n V:n v:n V:n

Figure A.21

4. One possibility: They may tend to seem to want to be able to understand.

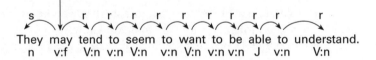

s r r r r r r r r r r
They may tend to seem to want to be able to understand.
n v:f V:n v:n V:n v:n V:n v:n v:n J v:n V:n

Figure A.22

7.3 5. Them, him, me, me, you. Object.

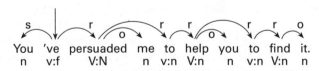

s r r r r r o
o o
You 've persuaded me to help you to find it.
n v:f V:N n v:n V:n n v:n V:n n

Figure A.23

7.4 6. *'ve*, because this is the word whose subject's position shows whether the sentence is a statement or a question, and because it needs 'she's in love' as its object – a kind of dependent.
7. *'s*, because the One-arrow Principle of Unit 3 prevents any word from depending on more than one other word, and *'s* is

the only word in 'she's in love' which doesn't already depend on some other word.

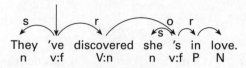

Figure A.24

7.5   8.   (a), (c): sharer, because *talking* and *to* are non-finite; (b), (d): object, because *likes* and *will* are finite.

9.

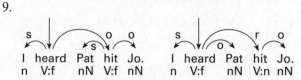

Figure A.25

7.6   10.   No. It's normally pronounced with a weak vowel and doesn't contrast with either *this* or *those*.

11.   See Figure 7.4.

12.   No.

7.7   13.   (a) (It was raining) and (we all felt miserable). (b) I suspect (they missed the train). (c) I hope that (the sun will come out soon). (d) (They missed the train) but (they're coming by bus).

14.   You know (that) I told her. I told her (that) you know. You know and I told her. I told her and you know.

15.   For example: I hope that you invited her and she's coming.

7.8   16.   (a) The object of *know* seems to be a noun, 'all the students . . .', but in fact it's the verb *like*. Solution: 'know that all . . .'. (b) *and* seems to coordinate the noun expansions 'a pot . . .' and 'a jar . . .', but really coordinates the clauses '. . . bought . . .' and '. . . turned up . . .'. Solution: '. . . honey, and . . .'. (c) The object of *believed* seems to be 'the reports . . .', which we apparently think are true; but then 'to be fashionable' seems to be the sharer, so we appear to think the reports are fashionable; but really 'the reports . . .' is the subject of *were*, and 'to be fashionable' depends on *attempts*! Solution: 'We all believed that the . . .' and 'in order to be . . .'.

17.   For example: (a) '. . . you that students . . .', '. . . that you students . . .'. (b) 'I heard that the . . .', 'I heard the president place/putting . . .'. (c) '. . . see that you . . .', '. . . see you in the same way as Pat'.

8.1 1. as, before, like, than, till, until.
2. If it has the same meaning in both patterns it must be the same word, so it must belong to the same word-class; and if its semantic relationship to the following word is the same, why not its syntactic relationship too? The fact that the same two possibilities apply to six other words supports this analysis against an analysis where the preposition *after* and the 'subordinating conjunction' (or whatever we call it) *after* just happen to have the same semantics.

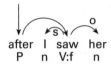

after I saw her
P   n V:f   n

Figure A.26

8.2 3. although, because, if, once, though, when, where, whereas, while.
4.

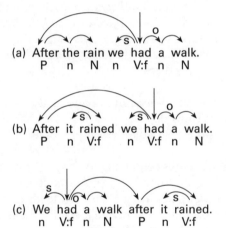

(a) After the rain we had a walk.
    P   n   N   n V:f n   N

(b) After it rained we had a walk.
    P   n V:f   n V:f n   N

(c) We had a walk after it rained.
    n V:f n   N   P   n V:f

Figure A.27

The verb that depends on the preposition is the one after it and nearest to it. The preposition depends on the other one, which may be either before or after it.

5. *are*.
6. *belong*. This is tricky because it's less obvious which word *for* belongs on; we shall sort this out in the next unit.

8.3 7. A pronoun, but it normally stands at the front of its clause rather than in its expected position (e.g. after *with* in examples (c) and (d). *who, whose, when, where, why* and *how*, plus *whoever*, etc.

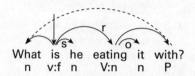

Figure A.28

You can't show that *what* depends on *with* because the arrow would tangle with the vertical arrow.

8. A noun – not a verb.

9.

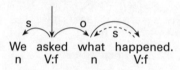

Figure A.29

What is the subject of *happened* (as in 'What happened?') but it must also be the object of *asked*, so it depends on two words. As we saw in Unit 3, this isn't normally allowed, so we show just the one dependency which is needed to hold the sentence together.

8.4 10. Yes: *when* and *where*. But these can also be used with a non-finite verb as dependent, which is a characteristic of some prepositions but no other wh-pronouns.

8.5 11. (a) I like books containing really. . . . (b) Walking down . . . I had . . . . (c) People living in . . . shouldn't. . . . .

12. (a) Books published before 1970 tended. . . . (b) . . . tasted nice baked in. . . . (c) Driven carefully, this car will. . . . (d) . . . all the students selected to. . . .

13. (a) I hope to see. . . . (b) I did it to please you. (c) . . . a book to read. . . . (d) A good book to read is. . . .

8.6 14.

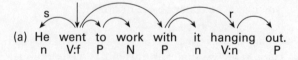

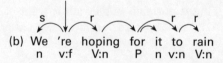

Figure A.30

9.1 1.

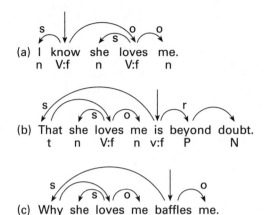

(a) I know she loves me.
 n V:f n V:f n

(b) That she loves me is beyond doubt.
 t   n   V:f n v:f   P   N

(c) Why she loves me baffles me.
 n   n   V:f n V:f   n

Figure A.31

2. How students are supposed to stay alive without getting into debt or working all hours of the day.

3. (a) [*Why* South . . . [*that* the . . . so strong [they have to be denied]]] remains to be seen. (b) [*That* the . . . [*when* preceded by a quantifier] is . . . background] is shown . . . essays [*written* in . . . Bali]. (c) You don't . . . genius [*to* see [*that* [*what* the economy needs] is . . . taxation [*to* solve . . . spending [(*which* will . . . election [*when* building . . . spent)]]]]].

9.2 4. (a) keen (b) ignorant (c) late (d) rejected (e) popular.

5. zero: [they recommended]; wh-pronoun: [which they recommended]; non-finite: [recommended].

6.

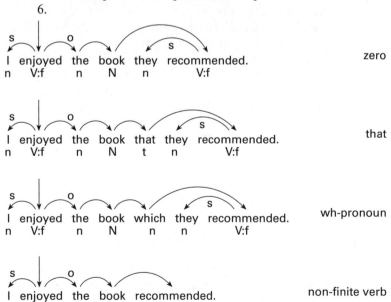

I enjoyed the book they recommended.   zero
n   V:f   n   N   n   V:f

I enjoyed the book that they recommended.   that
n   V:f   n   N   t   n   V:f

I enjoyed the book which they recommended.   wh-pronoun
n   V:f   n   N   n   n   V:f

I enjoyed the book recommended.   non-finite verb
n   V:f   n   N   V:n

Figure A.32

7.

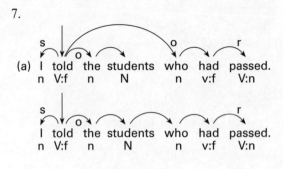

(a) I told the students who had passed.
   n V:f n   N   n v:f   V:n

I told the students who had passed.
n V:f n   N   n v:f   V:n

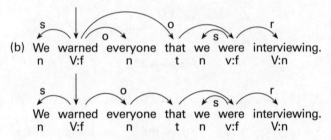

(b) We warned everyone that we were interviewing.
   n   V:f   n   t n v:f   V:n

We warned everyone that we were interviewing.
n   V:f   n   t n v:f   V:n

Figure A.33

9.3 8. (a) . . . ground [she walks on],' says Ted, [who had . . . Mary].
(b) . . . moment [he can]. . . . (c) . . . singers [who have . . .
voice]. (d) . . . Shirley Farmer [who wants . . . dies]. (e) . . .
friends [he had] . . . . (f) . . . correspondent [covering . . .
Britain]. (g) Applications [received after this date] . . . .

9.4 9. (a) afterwards, then (b) so, therefore (c) nevertheless (d)
meanwhile (e) noisily.

10. In each sentence the adverb clause can be at the end: 'We all
went home after that happened', etc.

11. I sleep well if before I go to bed I relax. If I relax before I go
to bed I sleep well. If before I go to bed I relax I sleep well.
The last strikes me as the hardest to understand, because the
dependencies are all piled up at the front of the sentence.

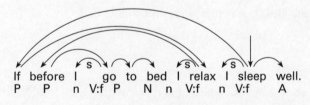

If before I go to bed I relax I sleep well.
P   P   n V:f P N n V:f n V:f   A

Figure A.34

12. *As* and *for* both depend on the second *are*.

13. (a) In . . . Catholics to respect gays, [*saying* [they can achieve
sanctity in the Church [if they abstain from sex]]]. (b)
Moments [after 10-year . . . Yorkshire], the flowerbeds . . .

crack [which rapidly . . . lagoon]. (c) [When a politician is on
song, [as Mr Major . . . yesterday]], the . . . stuff [it often is].
(d) [With no . . . drama], the Oklahoma . . . celebrities [to
match the glossy cast of the O. J. Simpson saga].

14.

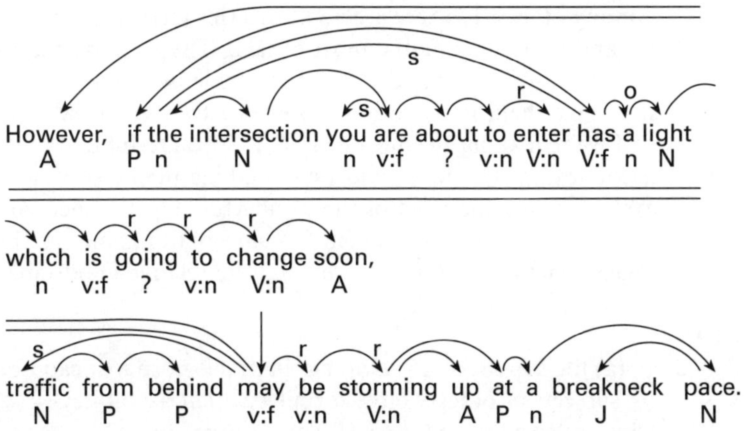

However,   if the intersection you are about to enter has a light
A   P n   N   n v:f ? v:n V:n V:f n N

which is going to change soon,
n   v:f ?   v:n   V:n   A

traffic from behind may be storming up at a breakneck pace.
N   P   P   v:f v:n   V:n   A P n   J   N

Figure A.35

10.1 1. (a) [Margery Manners], [one of . . . performers], died . . . . (b)
. . . for [her signature tune] ['Bring me the sunshine of your
smile'], which . . . (It may be best to treat the song title as a
single unanalysable proper noun.)
2. (a) Bill Clinton, the President of the USA, is . . . person. (Or:
The President of the USA, Bill Clinton, is . . . person.) (b)
My friend Fred is . . . tonight. (Or: Fred, my friend. . . .) (c)
That idiot Pat has . . . again. (d) The village of Skenfrith
nestles . . . hill. (e) Global temperatures are rising steadily, a
matter of great concern to us all.
3. They both refer to the same person or thing.
4. *Pat* depends on *my* (or maybe on *friend* – we can leave this
open), because this is the direction of dependencies in the
two clear cases: pronoun + common noun ('you students')
and common noun + *of* + village name ('the village of
Skenfrith').

10.2 5. (a) The fact [that it rained] . . . . (b) . . . the idea [that . . .
married]. (c) Your discovery [that . . . nouns] . . . . (d) . . . the
idea of [turning . . . round].

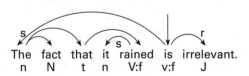

The fact that it rained is irrelevant.
n   N   t   n   V:f   v:f   J

Figure A.36

**UNIT 10
SENTENCES
AND
INFORMATION**

6. More flexible, because it allows us to use noun clauses just like ordinary nouns by making the noun clause depend on an ordinary noun. In all these sentences, the ordinary noun and its determiner (e.g. 'the idea') are essential; without them, the sentence is ungrammatical.

7. Among others: 1. There are no exams this term, it's wonderful and we're making the most of it. 2. There are no exams this term, which is wonderful, and we're making the most of it. 3. That there are no exams this term is true and wonderful, and we're making the most of it. 4. It's wonderful that there are no exams this term, and we're making the most of it. 5. We're making the most of the wonderful fact that there are no exams this term. I prefer 5 – no coordination, so the logical relationships are clearer, and the relative importance of the different parts is clearer.

10.3 8. In (a) the subject of *is* is *that*, but in b) it is *it*, so *that* can't be its subject; in other words, *it* replaces *that* as subject of *is*, which allows *that* to follow *is*. This change is possible for any noun clause used as subject (and for some others too).

9. *is*, though not as subject. It must depend on *is* because it takes its place among the dependents of *is* – more precisely, it has to be the last of these dependents. If this whole sentence is subordinated, the delayed *that* clause has to be attached to the same verb *is*, not to a higher one.

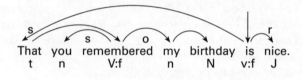

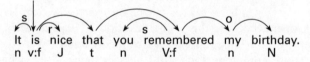

Figure A.37

10.

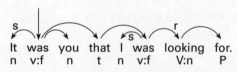

Figure A.38

11. Among others: 1. It was Pat that wrote . . . . 2. It was that essay that Pat wrote . . . . 3. It was for Jo that Pat wrote . . . . 4. It was on her PC that Pat wrote . . . . 5. It was last night

that Pat wrote .... . Each sentence focuses attention on a different idea, expressed by the noun after 'It was'.

12. (a) It's a shame [he's . . . here]. (b) It . . . impossible [to force myself to work] sometimes. (c) It's . . . miner [I feel sorry for], especially . . . family. (d) It is . . . achieve [which counts]. (e) It wasn't . . . thirty [that I . . . them].

10.4 13. *There*, because it follows all the usual rules for subjects – it normally precedes the verb, it follows the verb in a question, it cannot be omitted if the verb is finite, and so on. None of these things is true of *a*, though this is nevertheless a tempting candidate because its role in the meaning is so subject-like: the sentence means the same as 'A third strategy exists' (or even the rather odd 'A third strategy is'), where *a* is undoubtedly the verb's subject. If *there* is subject, it must be a noun (and more precisely it is presumably a pronoun). No, the two *there*'s are pronounced differently and have different meanings.

14. *Is* – there's no other word available! It can't depend on *there* because the arrow would tangle with the vertical arrow.

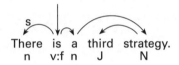

There is a third strategy.
  n   v:f n   J   N

Figure A.39

15. (a) When . . . there were [guards] there as well. (b) Are there [any . . . father]?   (c) There should be [quite . . . tomorrow].

10.5 16. Note: '#' stands for one of the punctuation marks , . : ; In order not to give away the answer to question 18 I haven't restored capital letters.

you . . . feeling # you . . . time # and . . . lives # everything goes smoothly # you . . . means # she . . . mean # you . . . things # what . . . rhythm # you feel wonderful # you're . . . right # and you . . . too # but you . . . too # you meet someone # you . . . them # to . . . impression # but . . . right.

17. It all depends on what syntactic links (dependency or coordination) hold two adjacent words together. If there are no such links, use a full-stop/period; if there is just coordination, use a comma.

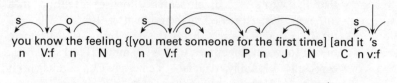

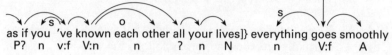

Figure A.40

18. (To avoid confusion missing words are shown by an under-line rather than dots.) You _: you _, and _. Everything _. You_; she _. What _. Your _. You _; you're _. And you _.

    But you _: you _, you _, to _, but _ wrong.

    Possible extra rules: (a) Choose your punctuation mark according to the importance of the boundary in terms of information from the following ranked list of punctuation marks ('>' means 'is more important than'): paragraph-indentation + '.' > '.' > ':' or ';' > ','. (b) Choose your punctuation mark according to the logical relationship between the words before it (X) and those after it (Y): use ':' if Y is an expansion of X, and ';' if it is an addition to X.

It is the contrast between dour, warren-like Victorian buildings
  v   N   N

and shiny new ones that gives the City its distinctive character.
              N   V   N   N

Though it hums with activity in business hours, few people have
         V   N   N   N   N   v

lived here since the nineteenth century.
 V   N

This pleasant small square has a paved centre
    J   J   N   V   J   N

with a flower stall and fountain depicting Venus.
      N N   N   V   N

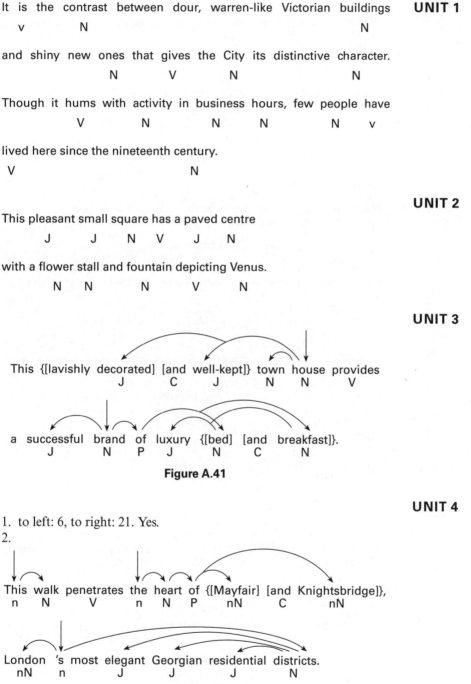

This {[lavishly decorated] [and well-kept]} town house provides
        J   C   J   N   N   V

a successful brand of luxury {[bed] [and breakfast]}.
J   N   P   J   N   C   N

Figure A.41

1. to left: 6, to right: 21. Yes.
2.

This walk penetrates the heart of {[Mayfair] [and Knightsbridge]},
 n   N   V   n   N   P   nN   C   nN

London 's most elegant Georgian residential districts.
 nN   n   J   J   J   N

Figure A.42

UNIT 5

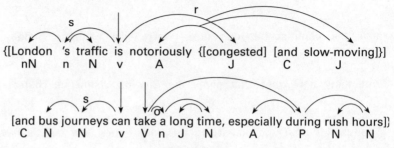

Figure A.43

UNIT 6

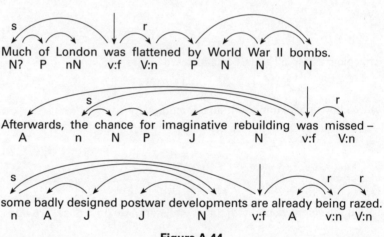

Figure A.44

UNIT 7

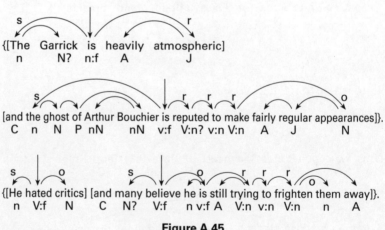

Figure A.45

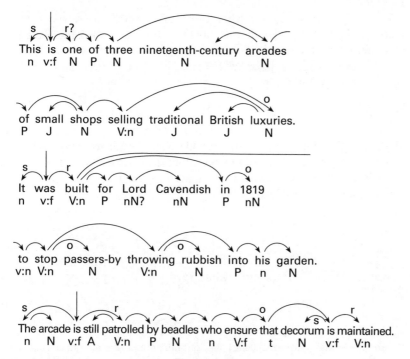

Figure A.46

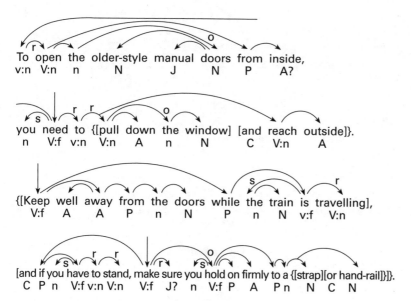

Figure A.47

Dear John,

I want a man who knows what love is all about. You are generous, kind, thoughtful. People who are not like you admit to being useless and inferior. You have ruined me for other men. I yearn for you. I have no feelings whatsoever when we're apart. I can be forever happy; will you let me be yours? Gloria

Dear John,

I want a man who knows what love is. All about you are generous, kind, thoughtful people who are not like you. Admit to being useless and inferior. You have ruined me. For other men I yearn; for you I have no feelings whatsoever. When we're apart I can be forever happy. Will you let me be? Yours, Gloria

UNIT 10

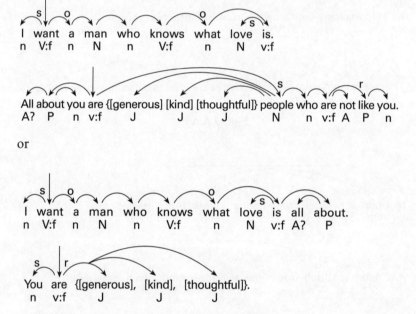

Figure A.48

REFERENCES AND FURTHER READING

Chalker, S. and Weiner, E. 1994. *The Oxford Dictionary of English Grammar*. Oxford: Oxford University Press.

Crystal, D. 1995. *The Cambridge Encyclopedia of the English Language*. Cambridge: Cambridge University Press.

Crystal, D. 1997. *The Cambridge Encyclopedia of Language*. Second edition. Cambridge: Cambridge University Press.

Fabb, N. 1994. *Sentence Structure*. London: Routledge.

Greenbaum, S. 1996. *The Oxford English Grammar*. Oxford: Oxford University Press.

Hudson, R. 1990. *English Word Grammar*. Oxford: Blackwell.

Hudson, R. 1992. *Teaching Grammar: A guide for the National Curriculum*. Oxford: Blackwell.

Hudson, R. 1995. *Word Meaning*. London: Routledge.

Jackendoff, R. 1993. *Patterns in the Mind*. Hemel Hempstead: Harvester.

Pinker, S. 1994. *The Language Instinct*. London: Penguin.

Quirk, R., Greenbaum, S., Leech, G. and Svartvik, J. 1985. *A Comprehensive Grammar of the English Language*. London: Longman.

Trask, L. 1993. *A Dictionary of Grammatical Terms in Linguistics*. London: Routledge.

Trask, L. 1995. *Language – the Basics*. London: Routledge.

REFERENCES

Further reading could take you in three different directions. 'English grammar' would take you further along the same track, with more details about more patterns. 'Theory of syntax' would be a rather different track, with a much deeper exploration of general questions that apply not only to English but to any language. 'Linguistics' is different again because it would involve even more general questions about language – not only to do with sentence structure but also to do with meaning, pronunciation, social influences, how children learn their first language and much (much) else. If you've coped with this book, you should be able to use any of the following, though some will make you work harder than I have! Please don't assume that books not on this list

FURTHER READING

aren't worth reading – they may be brilliant, and I may have simply forgotten about them (or not read them).

English grammar

Most of these books are for reference only, but you may find it fun to browse. The terms you know already will help you to find your way around, but most books list some individual words in their index, so you can use these as a guide.

- Quirk, Greenbaum, Leech and Svartvik (1985) – nearly 2,000 pages of facts, and still not complete!
- Greenbaum (1996) – about half the size of Quirk *et al.* (1985), and easier to use.
- Chalker and Weiner (1994). A very user-friendly, cheap and up-to-date guide to a thousand terms and ideas.
- Crystal (1995) *The Cambridge Encyclopedia of the English Language*. A brilliant and beautiful resource covering everything to do with English. The section on grammar is only forty pages long, but there are lots of mentions in other sections which are easy to find via the index.

Theory of syntax

This can be ferociously difficult but it doesn't have to be. You should be able to relate to the following:

- Fabb (1994). A companion workbook on sentence structure, aimed at people like you used to be before you used this book, but still useful because of its broader view over other languages.
- Trask (1993). Very user-friendly definitions of 1,500 terms used in modern syntax.
- Pinker (1994). Chapter 4 is a brilliantly clear introduction to Noam Chomsky's theory of sentence structure.

Most of the ideas in this book are quite commonplace, but the few that aren't are part of 'Word Grammar', a theory that I have described in a number of books. Hudson (1992) and (1995) are for beginners, but not all about syntactic theory; Hudson (1990) is all about syntactic (and semantic) theory, but not for beginners.

Linguistics

Linguistics is the study of language, so grammar is part of it. There are a host of readable introductions to linguistics.

- Jackendoff (1993). A clear and balanced presentation of some of the most interesting ideas in linguistics.
- Pinker (1994). A wonderful book, whose first fifty-eight words you now know very well indeed! At points where Noam Chomsky and his critics disagree he generally sides with Chomsky, so the book is controversial.
- Trask (1995). A very straightforward short introduction to the basic ideas of linguistics.
- Crystal (1997). Another brilliant and beautiful reference book which introduces the main discoveries of twentieth-century linguistics. Use it alongside Crystal (1995).

INDEX